Calgary LRT Walks: The South Stations

Thirty-Eight Walks - Eleven Stations

David Peyto

Peyto Lake Books

Published by Peyto Lake Books, Calgary, AB.
Email info@peytolakebooks.com
Website www.peytolakebooks.com

Printed and bound in Canada by Blitzprint, Calgary

Copyright 2013 by David Peyto

Library and Archives Canada Cataloguing in Publication

Peyto, David W., author
    Calgary LRT walks : the south stations / David Peyto.

"Thirty-eight walks—eleven stations".
Includes bibliographical references.
ISBN 978-0-9919150-1-9 (pbk.)

    1. Roads—Alberta—Calgary—Guidebooks.
2. Street-railroad stations—Alberta—Calgary—Guidebooks.
3. Calgary (Alta.)—Guidebooks. I. Title.

FC3697.67.P492 2013   917.123'38   C2013-902208-2

The front cover photos are Bow Valley Ranch House in Fish Creek Park and Rundle Ruins on 12th Avenue SE.
The back cover photo is in Union Cemetery.
All photos in the book unless otherwise indicated were taken by the author.

Dedication

This book is dedicated to my family.

Acknowledgements

It takes more than one person to create and publish a book. This book is no exception. I am fortunate to have the support of several people.

I want to thank my wife, Linda. As I developed the outline of this book I appreciated being able to share my ideas with her.

From the time I self-published my first book in 2002, my sisters, Margaret Peyto and Carol Cole, have been a tremendous support, taking the time to proof read the text for all my books and to provide me with positive suggestions.

Thank you to my brother-in-law, Ron Cole, and my nephews, Andrew, Ethan and Tim Cole, and my niece, Yolande Cole, for their support during the writing of my books.

Thank you to Blitzprint for their assistance with printing my books.

Thank you to Calgary Transit for their interest in this book.

Thank you to Glenbow Museum Archives for permission to use the historic photos in this book.

My decision to organize and write this type of walking guidebook was made after reading *Sky Train Explorer* by John Atkin. His book describes heritage walks from every station between Vancouver's Waterfront Station and the New Westminster Station.

Disclaimer

This book is a guide and should be used as such. Route conditions may change due to weather, lack of path or trail maintenance or other factors. *Calgary LRT Walks: The South Stations* reports conditions along each route at the time of writing but does not recommend whether or not you should go on each walk. It is necessary to plan ahead based on your ability and the weather. The author and publisher is not responsible for any loss, damage, expense, injury or any other liability whatsoever suffered by any person resulting directly or indirectly from using this guidebook. Please be aware that you are walking at your own risk.

Contents

Introduction

Calgary LRT Walks: The South Stations provides information about thirty-eight walks that start and/or finish at one of the eleven South LRT Stations. The chapters are arranged in the same sequence as the stations if you ride the train from the City Centre to the end of the South line. These stations are Victoria Park/Stampede, Erlton/Stampede, 39th Avenue, Chinook, Heritage, Southland, Anderson, Canyon Meadows, Fish Creek/Lacombe, Shawnessy and Somerset/Bridlewood.

This book is one of a series of Calgary LRT Walks books. *Calgary LRT Walks: The Northwest Stations* provides information about thirty-six walks that start and/or finish at one of the nine Northwest Stations. At the time of writing, the Tuscany Station on the Northwest line is still under construction. I am currently researching routes for additional books in this series. I hope the *Calgary LRT Walks* books will encourage readers to explore Calgary in a unique way. Thinking about the environment, you might leave your vehicle at home and use public transit.

Enjoy yourself as you head out on your explorations. You will have the opportunity to discover many facets of Calgary, walking past historic buildings in older communities, viewing works of art, visiting old and new parks and green spaces, stopping at viewpoints, exploring trails and wandering the sidewalks and pathways in some of Calgary's newer communities. You may want to walk more than one shorter route on the same day.

Each walk is written in a similar format. To assist the reader in deciding what walk to select there are brief notes for each route under the following headings.

Station Information: Each chapter begins with a physical description of the station and information about buildings and communities adjacent to the station.

Walk Overview: This section provides a description of the area in which the walk is located noting some of the more interesting locations along the route. These locations may include riverside pathways, natural areas, viewpoints, community parks or historic buildings. The walk may be a loop route, an out-and-back route, a linear route or a combination of these options. If a walk is in an isolated area this is mentioned in the text.

Length: This refers to the approximate distance for the walk (in kilometres).

Route Description & Accessibility: Information is provided about the accessibility of each route for users of wheelchairs or baby strollers. This description includes the type of walking surface – paved, sidewalks, gravel, dirt or grass. The level of difficulty (flat or gently rolling, small hills or steep ascents or descents) is also mentioned. On some walks an alternate route or detour with better accessibility is included in the text.

Food and Drink: Information is provided about parks, green spaces and viewpoints along or near the route where you can stop and enjoy your drink and lunch or snack. Information is also provided about coffee shops, grocery stores, convenience stores and restaurants located along or near the route.

Washrooms: This section lists the locations of washrooms in parks or public buildings along the route. Please remember that the washrooms in restaurants, coffee shops or stores are for customers only.

Map References: Map page numbers for each walk are given using the following map books as references. Walkers are encouraged to take the map book of their choice, or a Calgary Transit Map, or a Calgary Pathways and Bikeways Map, and this guidebook on each walk. Calgary Transit Maps and Calgary Pathway and Bikeways Map are available at any Calgary Public Library.
- Clearview – Clearview Map of Calgary 2011 Edition
- MapArt – MapArt Calgary & Southern Alberta – Large Print 2011 Edition
- Rand McNally – Rand McNally Calgary 2008 Edition
- Sherlock – Sherlock's Map of Calgary 14th Edition 2012

Route Category: The routes have been divided into four categories.

   Walk: This type of route starts and finishes at the station. The walk may be a loop, an out-and-back or a combination of both. There are fourteen South Stations walks in this category.
Victoria Park/Stampede 1, 2, 3, 4
Erlton/Stampede 1, 2, 3
39th Avenue 1, 2
Canyon Meadows 1, 2
Fish Creek/Lacombe 3
Shawnessy 1
Somerset/Bridlewood 1

   Bus/Walk: This type of route involves riding a bus from the station to the starting point of the walk. The walking route is then a linear walk ending back at the station. There are two South Stations walks in this category.
Fish Creek/Lacombe 1
Somerset/Bridlewood 2

   Walk/Bus: This type of route starts from the station and after a linear walking route there is a bus ride back to the station from the finishing point of the walk. There are no South Stations walks in this category.

   Bus/Walk/Bus: This type of route involves riding a bus from the station to the starting point of the walk. The walk might be a loop, an out-and-back, a linear or a combination. At the end of the walk there is a bus

ride from the finish back to the station. There are twenty-two South Stations walks in this category.
Chinook 1, 2, 3, 4
Heritage 1, 2, 3
Southland 1
Anderson 1, 2, 3
Canyon Meadows 3, 4, 5
Fish Creek/Lacombe 2
Somerset/Bridlewood 3, 4, 5, 6, 7, 8, 9

Bus Directions from the station to the start of the walk:
This section includes the four-digit bus stop number at the station and the four-digit bus stop number and its location at the start of the walk. The scheduled time for the bus to travel from the station stop to the stop at the start of the route, and the frequency of service for that route during mid-day (8:30 am to 4:00 pm) on weekdays and on Saturdays and Sundays is also included.

The Walk: This section describes the route in detail. In the text I have included the following terms. *Path* refers to any paved path or pathway. *Trail* includes any dirt, cinder or gravel surfaces. *Gateway* is used in the text to indicate an opening in a fence.

Bus Directions from the end of the walk to the station: This section includes the four-digit bus stop number and location for the bus stop at the end of the walk and the four-digit bus stop number for the stop at the station. The scheduled time for the bus to travel from the stop at the end of the walk to the stop back at the station, and the frequency of service for that route during mid-day (8:30 am to 4:00 pm) on weekdays and on Saturdays and Sundays is also included.

Route Summary: This section at the end of each walk summarizes the route directions.

What to take

The following items are recommended:
- A good pair of walking shoes or boots
- Clothing and a hat suitable for Calgary's very changeable weather
- Water or juice and lunch or a snack
- Train/bus fare money, a transit timetable and a Calgary Transit map
- A city map of your choice and this guidebook
- Sunscreen and/or insect repellent depending on the time of year
- A first-aid kit containing bandages, moleskin, tape, antiseptic ointment and a pair of folding scissors

- A camera and books about birds or flowers are optional
- Sunglasses
- A compass
- A backpack to carry everything

Transit Fares

At the time of writing an adult single fare is $3.00 and a youth single fare (6 to 14) is $1.75. Children under 6 ride for free. You can also purchase books of ten tickets ($30.00 for adults and $17.50 for youth). A day pass is $9.00 for adults and $5.75 for youth. A monthly pass costs $94 for adults and $57.50 for youth. Seniors over 65 can purchase a yearly pass for $95 beginning July 1st, 2013. The Calgary Transit website lists the fare vendors. The city-wide vendors include Calgary Co-op, Canada Safeway, Mac's Convenience Stores and 7-Eleven Food Stores. The downtown vendors include the Calgary Transit Customer Service Centre at 234 – 7th Avenue SW and City Hall Cashiers.

Calgary Transit Customer Service

The Calgary Transit website is www.calgarytransit.com
The Calgary Transit Call Centre phone number is 403-262-1000. The Transit Call Centre hours are 6 am to 9 pm on weekdays and 8 am to 6 pm on weekends and some holidays. Call for information on routes, schedules, fares and other services or let the Centre know if you have a commendation, suggestion, or concern about any of Calgary Transit's services.
The Teletype Number (TTY) for hearing impaired customers is 403-268-8087.
The Customer Service Centre at 234 – 7th Avenue SW has passes, tickets, information, route maps and schedules. It is open weekdays from 10 am to 5:30 pm. A second Customer Service Centre is located at 125- 7th Avenue SE beside the Centre Street Station platform. Lost property can be picked up at this location. Lost property phone inquiries can be made at 403-268-1600 on weekdays from 10 am to 5:30 pm.
The Access Calgary phone number 403-537-7770 is for inquiries about Access Calgary services.

How to Use Teleride

It is easy to connect with your Teleride bus stop numbers. Go to the bus stop that you use and record the four-digit Teleride bus stop number for your route. Call the Teleride phone number 403-974-4000 and enter your four-digit stop number. There are three types of information you can access to help you use Calgary Transit.

Press 1 to obtain current bus times (the next two or three buses). Call every day. Teleride tells you if there are any delays on your route caused by detours, construction, weather or traffic.

Press 2 to obtain future bus times (buses you want at a later date or time, up to a week in advance).

Press 3 to obtain general transit information on fares, special events, etc. All four-digit stop numbers for the station bus stops and the stops at the start and finish of walks are included in the text on the walks that require a bus.

Calgary Transit History

The Calgary Municipal Railway

The Calgary Municipal Railway (CMR) provided streetcar service to Calgarians from 1909 to 1950, a time that included World War I and II and the Great Depression of the 1930s. The CMR also operated Bowness Park.

Calgary Transit System

From 1947 to 1950 the newly-named Calgary Transit System began to phase out the use of streetcars combined with the introduction of electrically-powered trolley coaches. Gasoline and diesel-powered buses also began operating. On June 1st, 1947, the first trolley coach operated on the Crescent Heights route. On December 29th, 1950, the last streetcar travelled on the Ogden route. In 1970 the Calgary Transit System was renamed Calgary Transit. The trolley coaches stopped operating on March 8th, 1975.

LRT History

Route 201 (Red Line) presently operates from Crowfoot Station on the Northwest line to Somerset-Bridlewood Station on the South line. In 1979 construction began on a 12.5 km light rail transit line from 8th Street West downtown south to Anderson Road. The LRT made its inaugural run on this line on May 25th, 1981. In 1987 the Northwest line began operating from the University Station to Downtown. Three years later the Northwest line was extended to Brentwood Station. The South line was then extended two more stations to Canyon Meadows and Fish Creek-Lacombe Stations in 2001. In

2003 the Northwest line was extended one more station to Dalhousie Station. Another two stations were added to the South line in 2004 as the line was extended to Shawnessy and Somerset-Bridlewood Stations. Crowfoot Station on the Northwest opened in June 2009. Tuscany Station is scheduled to open in 2014.

Route 202 (Blue Line) is from 69th Street Station on the West line to Saddletowne Station on the Northeast line. In 1985 the Northeast line began operating between Whitehorn Station and 8th Street West Station. McKnight-Westwinds Stations Station on the Northeast line opened in 2007. Martindale and Saddletowne Stations on the Northeast line opened in August 2012. The six stations on the West line opened in December 2012 as part of Route 202 (Blue Line). Future plans include a Southeast line and a North Central line.

Stairs connecting Scotchman's Hill to Stampede Park

Chapter One
Victoria Park/Stampede Station

Station Information: The station is on the east side of Macleod Trail at 15th Avenue SE. It is the first station on the South line after leaving the downtown City Hall Station. The next station to the south is Erlton/Stampede Park Station.

In 2003 the communities of Victoria Park and Connaught joined together as Beltline Community District. The community association is called Beltline Communities of Victoria and Connaught Association. The community boundaries for Beltline are 17th Avenue on the south, 14th Street on the west, the CPR tracks on the north and the Elbow River on the east side. Stampede Park is part of Beltline. Within the community the four neighbourhoods are West Connaught from 14th Street West to 8th Street West, Connaught Centre from 8th Street West to 4th Street West, Victoria Centre from 4th Street West to 1st Street East and East Victoria from 1st Street East to the Elbow River. Most of the walks in Beltline will be included in the *Calgary LRT Walks: Downtown & West Stations* book. The walks from Victoria Park/Stampede Station include the neighbourhoods of Victoria Centre and East Victoria.

The area extending south from the CPR tracks to 17th Avenue and from 4th Street SW east to the Elbow River dates back to pre-1900. The expansion of Stampede Park north from 17th Avenue to 12th Avenue has resulted in the demolition of most of the homes east of Macleod Trail. There are still some warehouses and older commercial blocks on the northern fringe of the community east of Macleod Trail between 10th Avenue and 12th Avenue. West of Macleod Trail has also seen some changes as several high-rise condo buildings now tower over the area although there are still some older houses, apartments, older commercial blocks and warehouses.

The Calgary & District Agricultural Society held its first fair in 1886. Three years later, the society acquired 94 acres of land from the federal government with the Society turning over the land to the city in 1901 and leasing it back on a long-term basis. This land was given the name Victoria Park that same year, being named after the adjacent residential community. In 1912 Guy Weadick organized the first Calgary Stampede. The name of the annual event was changed to the Calgary Exhibition and Stampede in 1923.

The first Agricultural building on the grounds was constructed in 1919. Some of the first facilities in the park included a racetrack, rifle range, ball diamond, soccer and rugby fields. The Stampede Corral arena opened in 1950. Prior to this, events were held in the Victoria Arena. The park was

14

expanded to 114 acres in 1954. In 1959 the Big Four Building opened. The building was named for the four financial backers of the 1912 Stampede: Senator Patrick Burns, A.E. Cross, George Lane and A.J. McLean. In 1968 city council approved the extension north of the park boundary from 17th Avenue to 14th Avenue. In 1974 major changes saw the construction of a new grandstand and the relocation of the Indian Village from the area west of the Stampede Corral to the south side of the park by the Elbow River. The development of Kinsmen Elbow River Park was also begun. The park was renamed Stampede Park in 1975. The first phase of the Roundup Centre (now the BMO Centre) was completed in 1981 with an addition being added in 2000. Scotiabank Saddledome opened in 1983 prior to Calgary hosting the 1988 Winter Olympics.

At the time of writing major changes are again planned for the park as the area between 12th Avenue and 14th Avenue and alongside the Elbow River is developed. During the expansion phase there may be temporary route detours or slight changes to the described routes in this book.

Victoria Park/Stampede Station opened in 1981 as part of Calgary's first LRT line between downtown and Anderson Station. The station has stairs and escalators connecting the centre platform to the pedestrian overpasses. The far side of the west overpass that crosses the southbound track and Macleod Trail has stairs and a ramp down to ground level at 15th Avenue. The far side of the east overpass that crosses the northbound track has stairs and a ramp leading down into the west side of Stampede Park. There is also an enclosed walkway along the south side of the BMO Centre connecting the station to the Scotiabank Saddledome.

Victoria Park/Stampede Walk 1
Stampede Park & Elbow River Pathway

Walk Overview: This loop route starts and ends in Stampede Park with the middle portion of the walk following the Elbow River Pathway. In early July during Stampede Week there is an admission charge to enter Stampede Park.

Length: 4.1 km

Route Description & Accessibility: Most of the route is on paved pathways or pavement. The route is mainly flat with good accessibility although there are some short ascents/descents along the Elbow River Pathway.

Food and Drink: Some of the Stampede Park buildings have restaurants or food concessions available when the buildings are open to the public.

Washrooms: There are washrooms in some of the Stampede Park buildings when they are open to the public.

Map References: Clear-View – 29 & 37, MapArt – 164
Rand McNally – 50 & 60, Sherlock – 27 & 35

Route Category: Walk – The route starts and ends at the station (no bus is required).

The Walk: Exit the station at the upper level and turn left descending a set of stairs down into Stampede Park. There is a ramp nearby for better accessibility. The bottom of the stairs is on the west side of the BMO Centre. On the west wall of the BMO Centre is a large mural entitled *The Cowboy Chuckwagon Race* by artist Rocky Barstad. From the mural turn left and start walking north with the train tracks on the left and the BMO Centre on the right.

In a short distance you reach a corner of the BMO Centre. The benches in this area are back-to-back with replica metal wagon wheels on the ends and metal trim behind the back of the benches. A few steps north of the benches is Linda Stewart's bronze sculpture entitled *Roundup.* The sculpture has a cowboy on a horse following a calf.

From the sculpture, you walk in a northeasterly direction along the north side of the BMO Centre. Turn left walking past the west side of the Stampede Casino Building. On the right between the casino and 12th Avenue is Dafoe Terrace (0.4 km), constructed in 1910 by brothers John Dafoe and Alexander Norman Dafoe. This brick building with sandstone trim is a good example of the type of multiple housing buildings constructed in Calgary between 1906 and 1914. In 1987 Dafoe Terrace was declared a Provincial Historic Resource. The building is now within the boundaries of Stampede Park.

On the northwest corner of the intersection of 12th Avenue and 3rd Street kitty-corner from Dafoe Terrace is Fairey Terrace constructed circa 1903 by contractor Frank Fairey. When this brick building with sandstone trim first opened it contained twelve apartments. Fairey Terrace was also declared a Provincial Historic Resource in 1987.

A short distance west of Fairey Terrace is a rather dilapidated old house with the windows and doors boarded up. Enoch Sales, owner of the Sales Clothing Company, built this home in 1904. The building is the only home of its type still standing east of Macleod Trail in Victoria Park.

Former Westbourne Baptist Church building

From the corner at 3rd Street turn right and start walking east along 12th Avenue. On the right is the north side of the Stampede Casino. Two western theme sculptures entitled *The Ride* and *Courage and Thunder* by artists Veronica and Edwin Dam de Nogales are located on a cement wall in front of the casino.

On the north side of 12th Avenue between 3rd Street and Olympic Way (formerly 4th Street) major changes have taken place. For many years two school buildings and their adjacent playing field occupied this block. Victoria Park School, a three-storey sandstone school on the north side of the block along 11th Avenue, was constructed in 1903 with additions in 1907 and 1912. Today only the 1912 section of the building remains. The Calgary Board of Education ceased operations in the building in 1995. A charter school then leased the building for several years before it was sold to a developer in 2004. The 3rd Street Station Walk 2 – The Warehouses of 10th and 11th Avenues in the *Calgary LRT Walks: Downtown & West Stations* book will pass by the north side of the school. The smaller Victoria Bungalow School was built in 1919 on the northwest corner of the block at 11th Avenue and 3rd Street. The developers moved the building to its present location in the middle of the block along 12th Avenue facing the casino. The building is currently named The Guardian Presentation Centre. East of the two former schools where the school playing fields were located is the Arriva Condos, a high-rise condo building.

At the next corner you reach Olympic Way, the name now used for 4th Street from 10th Avenue to 14th Avenue. A new underpass on 4th Street between 9th and 10th Avenues offers a good alternate route for drivers to reach Stampede Park from north of the CPR tracks.

Turn right and walk one block south from 12th Avenue on Olympic Way to the former Westbourne Baptist Church built in 1910 on the northwest corner at 13th Avenue. This building is also now on Stampede Park property. The most well-known minister at the church was probably William Aberhart. He began his *Back to the Bible Hour* radio ministry from this building in the 1920s. Aberhart served as Alberta's premier from 1935 to 1943.

Retrace your steps back to 12th Avenue, turn right and continue east along 12th Avenue. On the southeast corner of 12th Avenue and Olympic Way a large information board shows the expansion plans for Stampede Park. Looking south from 12th Avenue at 5th Street, you can see the Stephenson Grocery building constructed in 1911 on the northeast corner of 13th Avenue and 5th Street.

North of 12th Avenue a few of the older Victoria Park homes still remain on 10th Avenue. The route passes Rundle Ruins on 12th Avenue just before 6th Street (1.1 km). The ruins are pictured on the front cover. A seniors' home named Rundle occupied this site from 1955 to 1971. The seniors' home was named for Methodist missionary, Robert Rundle, the first Protestant missionary in the area that became Alberta. He ministered in Southern Alberta from 1840 to 1848 before returning to England. Mount Rundle in Banff National Park and Rundle community in northeast Calgary are named after Rev. Rundle.

The sandstone remains are all that is left of Calgary's second General Hospital. The ruins include portions of additions added to the hospital in 1899, 1903 and 1905. Nothing remains of the original 1890 building. Hopefully Rundle Ruins, Stephenson Grocery building and the former Westbourne Baptist Church will be included in the Stampede Park expansion plans. East of the ruins is a ball diamond with Victoria Park community hall further south.

As 12th Avenue reaches the Elbow River, the road turns left to follow the riverbank and the name changes to 7th Street. In a short distance the route reaches Macdonald Bridge (1.4 km). This bridge and road may have been named for Canada's first prime minister or for one of several other individuals named Macdonald who resided in early Calgary. Cross the bridge and turn right onto the Elbow River Pathway. Near the parking lot on the far side of the bridge a second large information board shows the projected plans for this section of Stampede Park along the riverbank. The path just south of the bridge has already been widened as part of the River Walk project. When completed the River Walk will extend east from Centre Street

View of the Elbow River and
Scotiabank Saddledome from Macdonald Bridge

Sunshine Auto Camp ca. 1920. Glenbow Archives PA-2108-9

Bridge along the south side of the Bow River and turn south along the Elbow River to Lindsay Park.

This section of the route south from the bridge is an enjoyable walk. On the far side of the river is the former Weston Bakery (Golden West Bakery), a brick building constructed in 1929 and operated as a bakery until 1989. The

19

building is now owned by the Calgary Exhibition and Stampede. The information board by the parking lot shows that this building will become a Performing Arts Centre.

This section of the pathway is scheduled to undergo major changes as part of the expansion of the park. The Indian Village will be moved here from the south side of the park and Rotary House will be relocated here from just south of Stampede Station. A Heritage Trail will also be built in this area. At one time the Sunshine Auto Camp shown in the photo on the previous page was located in this area between the river and the escarpment slope.

The path goes under a traffic bridge and soon reaches a smaller bridge (2.0 km). On the left near this smaller bridge a set of stairs leads up the escarpment slope to the top of Scotchman's Hill. The route for Victoria Park/Stampede Walk 2 – Ramsay & Scotchman's Hill crosses this bridge and climbs the set of stairs.

The route continues south on the path from the smaller bridge to enter a narrow area sandwiched between the river on the right and the escarpment slope of Scotchman's Hill on the left. Please note that this section of path is isolated so use your own discretion about walking alone. There are large rocks enclosed in wire on the east side of the pathway to keep the lower portion of the escarpment slope from sliding onto the path. The path goes under two more bridges. A wire fence on the left separates pathway users from the stable area on the other side of the fence. At a junction turn right and continue walking beside the river as the path heads west on the north side of 25th Avenue (2.8 km). This area is where a railway line led to the former train station at 18th Avenue and 1st Street SW. The former station is on Victoria Park/Stampede Walk 4 – Mission and Cliff Bungalow.

The path soon reaches the area currently used as the Indian Village during Stampede Week. At a junction turn right through a gateway in the fence and follow the path to reach the 3rd Street Bridge at the south entrance to the park (3.4 km).

Turn right across the bridge and continue northbound, walking parallel to the WestJet Sky Ride from the nearby south terminal to the far north terminal of the ride just south of the BMO Centre. The Big Four Building on the left will be demolished as part of the expansion plans and replaced with a new exhibition building and a hotel. An amphitheatre will be built south of the present Big Four Building site. From the north terminal of the Sky Ride angle to the left and head back to the station (4.1 km).

The Weadickville area of Stampede Park named for Guy Weadick, promoter of the first Stampede in 1912, is west of the north terminal of the Sky Ride on the north side of the Big Four Building. Rotary House, a large log cabin building built in 1979, is the largest building in Weadickville. The building can be booked for weddings or other events and is especially busy during Stampede Week. Other buildings in Weadickville include an authentic 1885 homesteaders' cabin, an original North West Mounted Police barracks moved to Stampede Park in 1935 from Morley, and a former Stampede Post Office.

Route Summary:

1. Exit through the station doors at the upper level of the building and turn left descending a set of stairs down into Stampede Park.
2. From the front of the mural at the bottom of the stairs turn left and walk north with the BMO Centre on the right.
3. Angle to the right walking in a northeasterly direction with the BMO Centre still on the right.
4. Angle to the left walking north past Dafoe Terrace to the corner of 12th Avenue and 3rd Street.
5. Turn right and walk one block east on 12th Avenue.
6. Turn right and walk one block south on Olympic Way.
7. Retrace your steps back to 12th Avenue.
8. Turn right and walk east on 12th Avenue angling to the left on 7th Street as 12th Avenue ends by the river.
9. Cross Macdonald Bridge and turn right onto the Elbow River Pathway.
10. Walk south under a bridge and after passing a second bridge follow the path through a narrow green space between the river and the escarpment slope of Scotchman's Hill.
11. Continue south under two more bridges, make a right turn at a junction and head west on the north side of 25th Avenue.
12. At the next junction turn right and follow the path west to the 3rd Street Bridge.
13. Cross the bridge and follow the route of the WestJet Sky Ride to the north terminal just south of the BMO Centre.
14. From the terminal angle to the left and head back to the station.

Victoria Park/Stampede Walk 2
Ramsay & Scotchman's Hill

Walk Overview: The route has an out-and-back section in Stampede Park connected to a loop through Ramsay community. Points of interest include several historic buildings and the view from the top of Scotchman's Hill. In early July during Stampede Week there is an admission charge to enter Stampede Park.

Length: 7.4 km

Route Description & Accessibility: This route has poor accessibility. There is a long set of stairs that you ascend/descend on the steep escarpment slope of Scotchman's Hill on the west side of Ramsay. There is also a descent/ascent on the east side of the hill. No alternate route is included in the text. Most of the route is on pavement or sidewalks.

Food and Drink: There are benches at the top of Scotchman's Hill where you can relax and enjoy the view. Along the route you pass a couple of older corner stores, a small bakery and a couple of restaurants. Some of the Stampede Park buildings have restaurants or food concessions available when the buildings are open to the public.

Washrooms: There are washrooms in some of the Stampede Park buildings when they are open to the public.

Map References: Clear-View – 29 & 37, MapArt – 164
Rand McNally – 50 & 60, Sherlock – 27, 35, 36 & 28

Route Category: Walk – The route starts and ends at the station (no bus is required)

The Walk: Exit the station doors at the upper level and angle to the right. Walk down either a set of stairs or a ramp into Stampede Park. On the left at the bottom of the stairs on the wall of the BMO Centre is a large mural entitled *The Cowboy Chuckwagon Race* by Rocky Barstad.

From the bottom of the stairs/ramp angle to the right keeping first the BMO Centre and then the Stampede Corral on the left. The route passes a sculpture entitled *The Bronc Twister* by Richard Roenisch. You pass a second mural by Keith Holmes entitled *The Ceremonial Ride.* The mural shows the appearance of the Royal Canadian Mounted Police Ceremonial Ride at the Calgary Horse Show in 1914. The rather faded detail on this mural was restored for the Stampede's 100th Anniversary in 2012.

An elevated walkway between the station and Scotiabank Saddledome leads through the BMO Centre and then passes by the south side of the Stampede Corral. Keep walking parallel to the walkway along the south side of the Corral. Climb a set of stairs up to the walkway near the southeast corner of the Corral to view a large set of pictures on glass. *The Shell Olympic Walkway* shows the various sports and their venues as well as other aspects of the 1988 Winter Olympics held in Calgary and area.

Retrace your steps down the stairs and walk to the southeast corner of the Corral and turn left. Walk a few steps north to a large mural entitled *Calgary Stampede Historical Mural* on the east wall of the Corral. From the mural angle to the southeast to a large bronze sculpture entitled *By the Banks of the Bow* by Bob Spaith and Richard Roenisch. The sculpture depicts fifteen horses and two riders crossing the river.

The Cowboy Chuckwagon Race mural by Rocky Barstad

By the Banks of the Bow sculpture in Stampede Park

From the sculpture, walk east along the south side of the Scotiabank Saddledome. On the right is the agriculture building including the Victoria Pavilion, the former home of Stampede Wrestling. The route then angles to the left after passing the Saddledome and crosses a small bridge (0.8 km) over the Elbow River. At this point you cross the route of Walk 1 in this chapter. Angle to the right and climb the long set of wooden stairs up to the top of Scotchman's Hill. At the top of the escarpment the route is on Salisbury Street (1.0 km). There is an excellent view from the top of the escarpment.

Of trivial interest is that the name of this street changes to Salisbury Avenue north of 17th Avenue and to 6th Street south of Margaret Avenue. The origin of the Salisbury name is unknown. The Salisbury sidewalk stamp on the northeast corner of the intersection with Burns Avenue is spelled correctly. However, on the southeast corner the spelling is Salsbury. There is also an older sidewalk stamp for Burns Avenue on the southeast corner.

For many years, Calgarians have gathered at the top of Scotchman's Hill or Scotsman's Hill during Stampede Week for a free view of the chuckwagon races and the fireworks. The first name given to the escarpment was Fraser's Hill or Frazer's Hill. Angus Fraser was the second manager of the Hudson's Bay Company in Calgary.

Ramsay community east of the top of the escarpment is one of Calgary's older communities. In 1956 the communities of Brewery Flats, Burnsland, Grandview and Mills Estate joined together to form one community named Ramsay in recognition of William Thomson Ramsay, a land agent and property developer in early Calgary.

From the top of the stairs the route turns right and heads south on Salisbury Street and 6th Street to a viewpoint with a railing and benches (1.3 km). From this location there is a close-up view of Stampede Park and downtown Calgary and a long-range panoramic view of Calgary. At the bottom of the steep escarpment slope is the Elbow River.

From the viewpoint cross to the east side of 6th Street and turn left heading north on Ramsay Street. On the right is a large open park area that slopes downhill towards Ramsay School. The upper portion of the school can be seen from this location. The route passes a small building with a mural on the wall beside a covered skating rink. This rink design is unique to Calgary with the natural ice surface protected from weather by a roof. Continue along Ramsay Street, turn right onto Burns Avenue and start heading east down a hill. Make a right turn onto Alexander Street and then make a left turn onto Margaret Avenue. Of trivial interest is the number of streets in Ramsay with first person names. The names include Margaret, Alexander, Constance, Elizabeth, William, Adelaide and Maggie.

Two houses overlooking the Elbow River, 1912.
Glenbow Archives PA-2568-92

Margaret Avenue joins Spiller Road at the northeast corner of the Ramsay School field (2.0 km). Prior to the building of Macleod Trail over Cemetery Hill, Spiller Road used to be called Macleod Trail and was a main road leading south from downtown. The sidewalk stamp on the northwest corner of Margaret Avenue and Spiller Road still shows the name Macleod Trail.

Turn right on Spiller Road walking south past the front of Ramsay School. This three-storey sandstone school is one of four sandstone schools constructed in 1912. The building is similar in design to Sunalta and King George Schools. It is the only one of the remaining sandstone schools in Calgary that did not have an addition added. Continue south on Spiller Road to 24th Avenue. On the southeast corner is the other remaining sidewalk stamp showing Macleod Trail. However, note that the spelling of this 1929 stamp is McLeod.

Turn left and follow 24th Avenue east past the front of the former Riverside Iron Works complex constructed in 1927. In front of one of the buildings is a rather controversial sculpture entitled *Device to Root Out Evil* by Dennis Oppenheim. The sculpture is of an upside church with the steeple stuck in the ground.

The former ironworks plant on this site moved from the company's original site in Bridgeland/Riverside on Meredith Road just west of 4th Street NE. On the east side of the former steel plant is a coffee shop. Continue walking east on 24th Avenue to where it ends at 8th Street. A sidewalk stamp on the northwest corner reads Eight St East. This is one of several stamps in the community reading Eight rather than Eighth. Turn left and walk one block north on 8th Street to 23rd Avenue. There is no sidewalk on either side of this block so use caution. There are two older sidewalk stamps on the southeast and northeast corners of 23rd Avenue and 8th Street. Turn left and walk west one block on 23rd Avenue towards Spiller Road.

Just before you reach Spiller Road there is a small commercial building at 703 – 23rd Avenue. This building has had various uses over the years including a grocery store. At the time of writing the present occupant is a bakery. Turn right and walk north on Spiller Road to 21st Avenue. Turn right and walk east on 21st Avenue.

The route passes St Anne's Catholic Church built in 1958 at 830 – 21st Avenue (3.3 km). The first St. Anne's church, built in 1910, served as a parish hall from 1958 to 1966. East of the church is Tinchebray House (1913) at 922 – 21st Avenue. This two-storey brick building was the rectory for the Priests of St. Mary of Tinchebray who served at the adjacent St. Ann's Catholic Church. The building was then renamed St. Ann's Convent and housed several orders of nuns. In 1975 the building became Sunrise Residence, an addiction treatment centre. Today the building is Raido House, a shelter for homeless teenagers.

Continue east on 21st Avenue to 11th Street. The Shamrock Hotel dating back to the 1920s is on the southwest corner of the intersection. Turn left and walk north on 11th Street to 19th Avenue. The C.C. Snowden Oils building at 2010 – 11th Street was constructed in 1911. A few steps further north at 1902 – 11th Street is the former Western Steel Products Ltd building (1918) which is now the home of Ramsay Design Centre.

Turn left and walk west on 19th Avenue towards 8th Street. McKay Lodge at 1016 – 19th Avenue SE is named for CPR railway engineer Robert McKay and his wife Mary who built this three-storey brick house in 1911. They rented out rooms and called the building McKay Lodge. You pass the Alberta Corner Store built in 1912 at 922 – 19th Avenue. Turn right at 8th Street (a continuation of Spiller Road). Note the rather interesting fence made of stone and branches on the northeast corner. Walk north one block on 8th Street and turn right onto 18th Avenue. Walk two blocks east on 18th Avenue back to 11th Street.

Turn left and walk north one block to 17th Avenue. On the left at this corner is a tin covered warehouse at 1701 – 11th Street SE. The name Calgary Co-operative Fur Farmers Association is painted on the building. The building was constructed in 1912 as a warehouse for the Canadian Western Natural Gas Company. The Fur Farmers Association then used the building from 1940 until the 1970s. After being vacant for over twenty years the building is now used as artists' studios. Artpoint Gallery and Studios Society is located in another former warehouse just north of this corner on Adelaide Street.

There is no vehicle access between 11th Street and 17th Avenue. Turn left on the north side of the former Calgary Co-operative Fur Farmers Association warehouse and follow the sidewalk a few steps to reach the east end of 17th Avenue. Walk west a few steps on 17th Avenue to 10th Street. On the northeast corner is the Frank Block, first owned by Louis Frank. Sydney Cooper operated a grocery store in this building from 1923 to 1975. Since that time the building has had various occupants including a Buddhist monastery. Continue west one more block to 9th Street. On the northwest corner is the Nevler (Yorkshire) Block first owned by Jeremiah Nevler. He lived with his family on the second floor above the grocery. From 1936 to 1945 Mary Pevsner operated the Yorkshire Grocery. For a few years the building was called the Lesik Block.

At this point in the walk you can combine a refreshment break with a visit to an older grocery store. Walk west one block on 17th Avenue to the Black & White Meat and Groceries (4.9 km) built on the southeast corner of 17th Avenue and 8th Street in 1948. There are cement steps outside the store where you can sit and enjoy a few minutes rest.

Retrace your steps back along 17th Avenue and make a left turn onto 9th Street. As you stroll north towards 11th Avenue there is the opportunity to view many older homes. There are three older sidewalk stamps on the southwest, southeast and northwest corners of 11th Avenue and 9th Street. The stamp on the southeast corner reads 1911 while the other two dates are not very legible. Turn left at 11th Avenue and walk west one block to 8th Street. Make a right turn and walk north towards Macdonald Avenue. The route passes an older commercial block at 1048 – 8th Street. At 1040 – 8th Street is the three-storey brick Beaudry Block, also known as the Rogers Block, constructed in 1911. Leon Beaudry operated a grocery here until the mid-1920s. For many years the main floor had room for two commercial businesses. The three floors of this commercial building make it different from the mostly two-storey commercial blocks built in that era.

Continue north and turn left onto Macdonald Avenue. Make a left turn onto Maggie Street (5.6 km), named for Maggie Beattie, daughter of Wesley Fletcher Orr, the original owner of the land. Orr was mayor of Calgary in 1894, 1895 and 1897. This rather narrow and quaint street with small older homes is gradually changing character with the influx of larger infill houses in the past few years. Near the south end of Maggie Street make a right turn

(5.9 km) and climb up a charming little street called Bison Path to Bellevue Avenue. Bison Path almost appears to be an alley rather than a street. There are no sidewalks on Bison Path so use caution.

Cross Bellevue Avenue and follow Salisbury Avenue west one block to where it turns south at the top of the escarpment overlooking Stampede Park. The historic photo on this page was probably taken from a location near the north end of Salisbury Avenue. In the foreground of the photo is the former Calgary General Hospital (the present-day location of Rundle Ruins). In the middle left of the photo is Victoria School with Fairey Terrace to the left of the school. In the far background of the photo is the hill west of Sarcee Trail.

Walk south on the grass on the west side of Salisbury Avenue and then continue on Salisbury Street south of 17th Avenue until you reach the set of stairs at the top of the escarpment slope (6.4 km). The sidewalk stamp on the northeast corner of 17th Avenue is also misspelled Salsbury. From the top of the stairs retrace the earlier route back to the station (7.4 km).

Route Summary:

1. Exit through the station doors at the upper level, angle to the right and walk down either a set of stairs or a ramp into Stampede Park.
2. From the bottom of the stairs angle to the right keeping BMO Centre and then the Stampede Corral on the left.

Calgary, Alberta ca. 1910. Glenbow Archives NA-2267-2

3. Climb a set of stairs near the southeast corner of the Stampede Corral to view *The Shell Olympic Walkway*.
4. Retrace your route back down the stairs and turn left to view a mural on the outer east wall of the Stampede Corral.
5. From the mural angle to the southeast to view a large horse sculpture.
6. From the sculpture walk east along the south side of the Scotiabank Saddledome.
7. The route angles to the left around behind the Saddledome and crosses a small bridge.
8. Angle to the right and climb a long set of stairs to the top of Scotchman's Hill.
9. Turn right at the top of the stairs and walk south to a viewpoint platform with a railing and benches.
10. Cross to the east side of 6th Street and angle to the left heading north on Ramsay Street.
11. Turn right heading east on Burns Avenue and then turn right on Alexander Street.
12. Turn left and walk east on Margaret Avenue to Spiller Road.
13. Turn right and walk south on Spiller Road to 24th Avenue.
14. Turn left and walk east on 24th Avenue to 8th Street.
15. Turn left and walk one block north on 8th Street.
16. Turn left and walk west on 23rd Avenue to Spiller Road.
17. Turn right and walk northeast on Spiller Road turning right on 21st Avenue.
18. Walk east on 21st Avenue to 11th Street.
19. Turn left and walk north on 11th Street to 19th Avenue.
20. Turn left and walk west on 19th Avenue to 8th Street.
21. Turn right and walk north on 8th Street.
22. Turn right and walk east on 18th Avenue to 11th Street.
23. Turn left and walk north on 11th Street.
24. Turn left at 17th Avenue and walk west to 8th Street.
25. Retrace your steps back to 9th Street, turn left and walk north to 11th Avenue.
26. Turn left and walk west on 11th Avenue to 8th Street.
27. Turn right and walk north to Macdonald Avenue.
28. Turn left on Macdonald Avenue and then left onto Maggie Street.
29. Follow Maggie Street south and turn right on Bison Path.
30. Climb Bison Path, cross Bellevue Avenue and follow first Salisbury Avenue and then Salisbury Street west and south back to the top of the stairs you climbed earlier.
31. Retrace the earlier route back to the station.

Victoria Park/Stampede Walk 3
Mission 2nd & 4th Streets

Walk Overview: This route combines an out-and-back section along 17th Avenue connected to a loop along 2nd and 4th Streets. Points of interest include the former Holy Cross Hospital site, the Elbow River Promenade, several historic buildings and some interesting artwork. Along 4th Street you can explore a variety of shops, coffee shops and restaurants. If you enjoy people-watching 4th Street is one of the better locations in the city. Another interesting feature is the blue street signs showing both the present numbered streets or avenues and the original names for these streets or avenues. East of 4th Street the original avenue names were of French origin and west of 4th Street the original streets were named after Canada's Governor Generals after Confederation in 1867.

Length: 3.7 km

Route Description & Accessibility: This flat route has good accessibility on a walking surface that is mostly sidewalks.

Food and Drink: There are benches by the Elbow River on 26th Avenue. On the second half of the walk the route passes numerous coffee shops and restaurants along 4th Street and on 17th Avenue.

Washrooms: There are no public washrooms along the route. The washrooms in restaurants, stores and coffee shops are for customers only.

Map References: Clear-View – 36, MapArt – 164
Rand McNally – 60 & 59, Sherlock – 27 & 35

Route Category: Walk – The route starts and ends at the station (no bus is required)

The Walk: Exit the station building at the upper level, turn right and cross the pedestrian overpass above the train tracks. Take a set of stairs on your left down to street level on the east side of Macleod Trail and walk south one block to 17th Avenue. Use the traffic lights at 17th Avenue to reach the southwest corner of 17th Avenue and Macleod Trail.

Begin walking west along 17th Avenue. In the 1940s the two blocks between Macleod Trail and Centre Street were mostly houses. In the first block several of these older houses have been converted to businesses. You pass a casino on the left at 1st Street SE. Note the two lion sculptures by the front entrance. The use of lion sculptures was very popular in Calgary prior to 1920.

Continue west along 17th Avenue towards 2nd Street SW. In the 1940s 17th Avenue between Centre Street and 4th Street SW was mainly residential with only a few businesses. On your left at 1st Street SW is Rouleauville Square (0.6 km), a 0.2 hectare plaza park created by closing 1st Street from 17th to 18th Avenues. On the north side of the square is a brick wall with a hand-sculptured mural. Walk 4 – Mission & Cliff Bungalow in this chapter follows a route along 18th and 19th Avenue past St. Mary's Cathedral and several other significant buildings. The FCJ Centre on 19th Avenue is also on the mural. In the centre of the mural are the Rouleau brothers, Charles and Edward. On their left is the former St. Mary's Parish Hall (CNoR Station) that is also on the Mission & Cliff Bungalow walk. The first St. Mary's High School is also shown. A set of interpretive signs in the Square provide historical information about the Cathedral Architecture, French at the Elbow River, French Settlement, Commerce, Health Care, Education, the Rouleau Legacy and Our Lady of Peace Mission. On the Mission & Cliff Bungalow walk the route will pass additional interpretive signs on the south side of the former St. Mary's Parish Hall.

From Rouleauville Square continue west along 17th Avenue, formerly known as Notre Dame Avenue. The Costigan Residence at 221 – 17th Avenue SW was built in 1894 by Calgary's first crown prosecutor, John Costigan, and his wife Ada. In 1928 the building was moved from its original location on the northwest corner of 1st Street and 17th Avenue SW to the present location. A nightclub presently occupies the building.

There are two interesting buildings at the corner of 2nd Street SW (Hamilton Street). On the northeast corner is the former Jacques Funeral Home building constructed in 1936. Owners of the building continued to use the Jacques Funeral Home name until the 1990s. First Memorial Funeral Services are the present occupants of the building. On the northwest corner of the intersection is the Model Milk Company building. This building with its distinctive milk bottles sculptures was constructed in 1934 with additions built in 1936 and 1958. Palm Dairies purchased the Model Milk Company in the 1960s.

From this corner turn left and walk south along 2nd Street SW. After you cross 18th Avenue (St. Joseph Avenue), St. Monica School is on the left. The school's patron, Saint Monica (331-387), the mother of St. Augustine, is the patron saint of married women. Her pagan husband, Patricius, had led a very immoral lifestyle filled with anger. Monica's dedication to prayer resulted in the conversion to Christianity of both Patricius and his mother.

On the southeast corner of the intersection of 2nd Street and 18th Avenue is a Centennial Obelisk. The 13.6 metric tonne structure was moved to this

Mural at Rouleauville Square

location in January 2012 from its previous location beside the former Catholic Office Building at 6th Avenue and Macleod Trail. In 1975 Catholic students created 7.5 cm by 7.5 cm clay tiles that were attached to either this 7.3 metre tall obelisk or along a low wall next to the former office building.

Continue south past 19th Avenue (St. Mary's Avenue). Our Lady of Lourdes School is on the left. This building is on the site of the original St. Mary's School built in 1909. A hard fought campaign to save the older building failed. The present structure that opened in 2005 is built in a similar style to the 1909 school and includes the sandstone façade and the original engraved name of St. Mary's from the first building. In 1918 the original building became St. Mary's Girls School when the boys were moved to a separate building nearby. In 1957 St. Mary's Boys School opened in the 100 block of 18th Avenue SW. When the girls were moved to the newer building in 1969 the name changed to St. Mary's School. The old school building then became a pastoral centre and day care until 1995 when it sat vacant until the controversial demolition in 2002.

Our Lady of Lourdes School offers a day treatment program focused on meeting the wide range of needs of students in grades 1 to 12 prior to the student returning to a regular school setting. The school name is derived from Bernadette Soubirous, a poor peasant girl who witnessed an appearance of the Blessed Virgin in 1858 near Lourdes, France. Lourdes is a famous pilgrim site. East of Our Lady of Lourdes School is Sacred Heart

Convent. This building is also on the Walk 4 – Mission & Cliff Bungalow route.

Continue south on 2nd Street past 20th Avenue (Oblate Avenue). The avenue was named for the Oblate Fathers who ministered in the area that became Alberta. Lacombe Avenue, the original name of 21st Avenue, is named for Father Albert Lacombe, an Oblate priest who established St. Albert and the Lacombe Home in Midnapore. He served as a priest in Western Canada for almost seventy years. Father Lacombe High School in Radisson Heights is also named in his honour. The Oblates of Mary Immaculate order began in France. In the middle of the 19th Century they began ministering in Western Canada.

Flexford House, a two-storey six-suite brick and sandstone apartment building constructed in 1915, is on the northwest corner of 21st Avenue. Percy Simons, a former NWMP officer and a bridge-builder, owned this site from 1904 to 1914. The contractor was Charles Lindsay. He operated a real estate partnership with his brother Thomas. The brothers were not related to Dr. Neville Lindsay for whom Lindsay Park is named.

Note the old blue street name on the corner of the building. There are very few of these old address signs left on buildings. The sidewalk stamp on the northeast corner of this intersection is dated 1913. This is the only older sidewalk stamp in Mission. On your left, just east of 2nd Street at 21st Avenue, a pedestrian bridge crosses the Elbow River into the west side of Lindsay Park. Walk 4 – Mission & Cliff Bungalow crosses this bridge.

Your route continues south on 2nd Street. Just beyond Holy Cross Lane on your left is the Holy Cross Hospital complex at 2210 – 2nd Street. Four Sisters of Charity, members of the Order of Grey Nuns based in Montreal, opened a small two-storey wooden structure in 1891 with a capacity of four patients. The following year a three-storey brick and sandstone building was constructed on this site on land donated by the Oblate Fathers. The 1892 building is shown in the photo on the next page. The Holy Cross Nursing School operated from 1907 to 1979. The 1928 addition is the oldest standing portion of the present building with the remainder being additions made in the 1950s and 60s. The Grey Nuns sold the hospital to the provincial government in 1969. In 1996 the building came under private ownership and is now occupied by clinics and offices. The Grey Nuns order was founded in the 1740s by Saint Marguerite d'Youville, the first Canadian born saint.

The former street names of 22nd Avenue and 23rd Avenue are Doucet Avenue and Rouleau Avenue respectively. Father Leon Doucet arrived in Canada from France in 1868, spending a short time in the St. Albert area before moving further south to minister to the Siksika people.

33

Holy Cross Hospital, ca. 1900-05. Glenbow Archives NA-920-3

Nuns and Nightingales Sculpture

Doucet was living along the Elbow River when the NWMP arrived in 1875. Father Doucet School is located in Shawnessy. Rouleau Avenue is named for brothers Charles and Edward Rouleau. Charles served as a chief justice of the Supreme Court in the North-West Territories. Edward was the chief surgeon for the North West Mounted Police. The village of Rouleauville south of 17th Avenue was annexed by Calgary by 1907.

On the front lawn near the 1928 structure is a sculpture entitled *Nuns and Nightingales*. This 2011 sculpture of a nun and a nurse by Shirley and Don Begg commemorates the Sisters of Charity (Grey Nuns) who established the hospital in 1891, and the graduates of the Holy Cross School of Nursing. On the wall of the 1928 building just south of the sculpture are the dates 1891 and 1928.

From the hospital continue walking south on 2nd Street past 24th Avenue (Grandin Avenue) to 25th Avenue (Scollen Avenue). Bishop Vital Grandin, ordained to the Order of Mary Immaculate in 1854, became a bishop three years later and was appointed bishop of St. Albert in 1871. Bishop Grandin High School is in Haysboro. Constantine Scollen, born in Ireland, was the first English-speaking priest in Alberta and the first teacher in Alberta. Father Scollen worked closely with Bishop Grandin and Father Lacombe. Father Scollen School is in Temple.

On the southeast corner at 25th Avenue are the Strand Apartments, built in 1920. Walk one more block south on 2nd Street and cross to the south side of 26th Avenue (1.7 km). Turn right and walk west along the Elbow River Promenade passing several interpretive plaques about Mission and Cliff Bungalow.

The modest brick house at 228 – 26th Avenue is the Lang House constructed in 1910 by architect George Lang. Lang and his partners designed several significant Calgary buildings including Firehall No. 1, Christ Church in Elbow Park and the Ogden Hotel (Alyth Lodge).

At the west end of the promenade is the north end of Mission Bridge at 4th Street. On the far side of 4th Street is the beginning of Elbow Drive. Mission Bridge, the oldest surviving concrete bridge in Alberta, was the first of three reinforced-concrete bridges built in Calgary between 1915 and 1921. Centre Street Bridge was built in 1916 and Louise (Hillhurst) Bridge in 1921. All three concrete bridges replaced steel bridges.

The route now turns right and heads north along 4th Street (Broadway Street). This section of the walk passes an interesting collection of shops, restaurants and coffee shops. On this street in the 1940s you might have stopped for a coffee at either the Top Hat Coffee Shop (2210 – 4th Street) or The Koffee Counter (2020 – 4th Street). You could also have stopped in at either the Little Gem Confectionary (2002 – 4th Street) or O'Rusty's Confectionary (2120 – 4th Street). You may find yourself crossing back and forth across 4th Street to view various points of interest.

From about 1884 to 1970 a very interesting building was located on the southeast corner of 4th Street and 25th Avenue. The former Blue Rock Hotel building was first used as a clubhouse for the Calgary Pigeon Shooting Club.

The Blue Rock Hotel then occupied the building from 1893 until after World War I. Later occupants were the Canada Laundry and Adanac Tile and Marble Company. Three notable buildings that have disappeared from 4th Street over the years are the Zelda Apartments (2406 – 4th Street), the Iris Block (2315A – 4th Street) and the Lenore Block (2309 – 4th Street).

There is also an interesting collection of sculptures along 4th Street as far north as 13th Avenue. *Welcoming the Sentinels of Time* by Fred Spina is on the southeast corner of 24th Avenue. The sculpture is comprised of 15 foot high wooden figurines.

The first historic building you pass is the Inglis-McNeill (Mission Cycle) building at 2310 – 4th Street. The building features a 1950s storefront addition added to a two-storey wood frame house. Mission Cycle, started by Henry Cheal in 1927, moved into the Inglis-McNeill building in 1955 after being in the Blue Rock Hotel building and in a building at 2414 – 4th Street. Mission Cycle closed in 2003 after 79 years in the Mission community. The store sign can still be seen in front of the building.

The next historic building of note is the Bannerman Block at 2306 – 4th Street. This two-storey brick building, with storefronts on the main floor below apartments, was built in 1911. On the next corner at 22nd Avenue is the Wright Block (Aberdeen Apartments) built in 1911. Dr. Harry Wright constructed this two-storey brick building with main floor storefronts and apartments upstairs. The building was renamed the Aberdeen Block or Aberdeen Apartments about 1917. The third of the three older commercial blocks on 4th Street is the Young Block constructed in 1912 at 2118 – 4th Street by printer James Young. Over the years the building's tenants have included a pool hall, groceries, beauty parlours, barbershops and restaurants.

The final historic building of interest is the Tivoli Theatre at 2015 – 4th Street, constructed in 1937 and closed as a theatre in 1990. Today the Tivoli Shops occupy the building. On the southwest corner across from the Tivoli is a steel and sheet metal sculpture entitled *Hanging Out* by Peter Smith. The sculpture is of three 10-foot high frogs relaxing on a bench.

Continue north on 4th Street. On the southeast corner of 19th Avenue is the sculpture entitled *Scene and Heard on Fourth* by Terry Gregoraschuk. The steel sculpture features four cows and a dog heading south along 4th Street. On the northwest corner of the same intersection is *Angel Heart* by Errol Lee Fullen. On the southeast corner of 18th Avenue is *Tree Houses* by Rick Silas. The final sculpture you will pass on 4th Street is *Starting Fourth* by Garry Jones on the southeast corner of 17th Avenue (2.8 km). This sculpture is a group of seven human-like figures clustered together. From the corner of 17th Avenue and 4th Street turn right and head east retracing your earlier route from 2nd Street SW back to the station at Macleod Trail (3.7 km).

Route Summary:

1. As you exit the station building at the upper level turn right and cross the pedestrian overpass above the train tracks and take a set of stairs on the left down to street level on the east side of Macleod Trail.
2. Walk south a few steps to the traffic lights and cross to the southwest corner of 17th Avenue and Macleod Trail.
3. Walk west on 17th Avenue to 2nd Street SW.
4. Turn left and walk south on 2nd Street to 26th Avenue.
5. Turn right and walk west to 4th Street.
6. Turn right and walk north to 17th Avenue.
7. Turn right and walk east on 17th Avenue back to Macleod Trail and the station.

Victoria Park/Stampede Walk 4
Mission & Cliff Bungalow

Walk Overview: This linear route meanders along streets in the adjacent communities of Mission and Cliff Bungalow where many of the older homes still remain. Short sections of the route are included in Victoria Park/Stampede Walk 3 – Mission 2nd & 4th Streets or Erlton/Stampede Walk 2 – Cliff Bungalow. Highlights in the early portion of the walk include the area around Rouleauville Square with St. Mary's Cathedral, the former St. Mary's Parish Hall/Canadian National Railway Station and the FCJ Centre. Near the end of the walk you visit Lindsay Park and the Talisman Centre.

Length: 5.7 km

Route Description & Accessibility: There is good accessibility for most of this route. The most challenging location is a short uphill section in Lindsay Park from the Elbow River Pathway to reach the former railway bridge on the north side of the park. The walking surface is a mix of sidewalks and paved paths.

Food and Drink: There are picnic tables and benches in Lindsay Park. Along the route you pass by numerous coffee shops or restaurants along 4th Street. There is a food concession in the Talisman Centre.

Washrooms: Near the end of the route there are washrooms in the Talisman Centre in Lindsay Park. The washrooms in restaurants, stores and coffee shops are for customers only.

Map References: Clear-View – 36, MapArt – 164
Rand McNally – 60 & 59, Sherlock – 27 & 35

Route Category: Walk – The route starts and ends at the station (no bus is required).

The Walk: At the upper level of the station turn right and cross the pedestrian overpass above Macleod Trail. On the west side there are stairs and a ramp leading down to ground level on 15th Avenue. Walk west on 15th Avenue to the MacDonald (Mount Royal) Apartments built in 1911 at 215 – 15th Avenue SE by James MacDonald, a builder and the president of MacDonald Oil Co. Ltd. The building is a U-shape surrounding a courtyard area in front of the main entrance.

Continue west on 15th Avenue crossing 1st Street SE and walking a few steps further west to the Colgrove Apartments at 129 – 15th Avenue SE. This three-storey brick building, constructed in 1912, has wooden verandahs on the front. A short distance further west at 117 – 15th Avenue SE is the Powell Block, a two storey commercial building with apartments above the main floor. Keep walking west on 15th Avenue and turn right onto Centre Street. On the left at 1411 Centre Street are the Healy Apartments, another older apartment building. Retrace your steps back to 15th Avenue and turn right walking west to 1st Street SW.

Turn left and walk south one block to 17th Avenue. Cross to the south side of the block and enter Rouleauville Square (0.8 km). This small park was developed when 1st Street SW was closed between 17th and 18th Avenues. A series of information signs outlines the history of the Rouleauville/Mission area. Walk 3 in this chapter also visits this park.

From the south side of the square angle to the left to the three-storey sandstone St. Mary's Parish Hall/CNR Station on the southeast corner of 18th Avenue and 1st Street SW. The building was constructed in 1905 as a parish hall for St. Mary's. In 1911 Canadian Northern Railway (CNoR) purchased the building and converted it into a station. The railway built an addition on the south end. The Canadian National Railway took over the operation of Canadian Northern Railway and continued to use the station until their passenger service to Calgary ended in 1971. In 1978 the City of Calgary purchased the building. When Alberta Ballet became the tenant of the building in 1985 the name was changed to Nat Christie Centre. On the southwest corner of 18th Avenue and 1st Street SW is St. Mary's Cathedral built in 1955-56. The original cathedral built in 1889 is shown in the photo on the next page.

Walk south on 1st Street towards 19th Avenue. On the left behind the train station is the Rouleau House built about 1887. The house was moved to this site in 2009 from 114 – 18th Avenue SW (Lot 29). The house had originally been built on Lot 27 and was first moved between 1900 and 1908. Dr. Edouard Rouleau moved west in 1887 from Quebec to join his older brother,

Judge Charles Rouleau. Dr. Rouleau was a very active member of the community.

On the south side of the relocated Rouleau House are two information signs about railways. The nearby former train bridge (now a pedestrian bridge) crosses the Elbow River to Lindsay Park. You will cross this bridge near the end of this walk.

The route now heads west along 19th Avenue behind the back of the cathedral. On the left is the Sacred Heart Convent built in 1893 by the Sisters of the Faithful Companions of Jesus (FCJ) who arrived in Calgary in

St. Mary's Church, 1905. Glenbow Archives NA-1497-8

Canadian Northern Railway Station, 1913-18.
Glenbow Archives ND-8-307

Athlone Apartments at 330 – 19th Avenue

1885. A two-storey frame building was constructed as a mission on this site in 1882. The frame building was demolished in 1924 when the east wing was added to the 1893 building. A chapel was added on the south side that same year. The building is now used for retreats and conferences.

Continue west along 19th Avenue crossing 2nd Street SW and walking west towards 4th Street. You pass the Athlone Apartments, a two-storey, forty-six units apartment building, constructed in 1940 at 330 – 19th Avenue SW. This building may have been named for Alexander Cambridge, Earl of Athlone (1874-1957), who served as governor-general of Canada from 1940 to 1947. He was married to Princess Alice, a granddaughter of Queen Victoria.

At 4th Street (1.4 km) cross to the west side of the street, turn right and head north to 18th Avenue. Turn left and walk west on 18th Avenue towards 5th Street SW. You pass the Red Cross Children's Hospital # 1, a two and one-half storey building, constructed in 1914 as a double residence at 522 – 18th Avenue SW. The Alberta Division of the Red Cross Society operated a children's hospital in the building from 1922 to 1929. The building then reverted to its earlier residential use.

At 5th Street turn left and walk one block south to 19th Avenue. Turn left and follow 19th Avenue east to 4th Street. You pass another older apartment building, the Robinette Apartments, at 510 – 19th Avenue SW. Turn right and walk south one block to 20th Avenue. Again turn right and walk one block west on 20th Avenue to 5th Street (2.2 km). Turn left and head south one block and turn left onto 21st Avenue. Follow 21st Avenue east to 2nd Street. Turn right and walk one block south on 2nd Street to 22nd Avenue.

Turn right and follow 22nd Avenue west to Cliff Street (3.3 km). On the west side of Cliff Street is Cliff Bungalow School. This building is described in more detail in Erlton/Stampede Walk 4 – Cliff Bungalow. Walk one block south on Cliff Street and turn left onto 23rd Avenue. Follow 23rd Avenue east to 2nd Street. At this point you will be facing the former Holy Cross Hospital building on the east side of 2nd Street. The hospital is described in more detail in Victoria Park/Stampede Walk 3 – Mission 2nd and 4th Streets.

Turn right and walk one block south on 2nd Street and turn left onto 24th Avenue. Walk east one block on 24th Avenue towards 1st Street. On the right is William Aberhart Park. Aberhart was premier of Alberta from 1935 to 1943. There are benches in the park. On the east side of the park is a community garden. Turn left and follow 1st Street SW (Jean Baptiste Street) north to where it ends beside the Elbow River. Follow Holy Cross Lane, a small street angling to the left away from 1st Street. When Holy Cross Lane turns left to head towards 2nd Street turn to the right and follow a path beside the river to reach the pedestrian bridge leading across the river to Lindsay Park (4.6 km).

Cross the bridge and take the path to the left. Please note that this path through the park is isolated so use your own discretion about walking alone. The path leads along the edge of the river to the former train bridge across the river (4.8 km). Climb a set of wooden stairs, cross the bridge and angle to the left to the corner of 19th Avenue and 1st Street SW where you were standing earlier by Rouleau House. A pathway on the east side of the bridge provides better accessibility up to the bridge than the wooden stairs.

Walk north on 1st Street and turn right onto 18th Avenue. St. Mary's High School is a short distance east on the right. Facing the school at 110 – 18th Avenue SW is the McHugh House built about 1896. The brick building is the former home of J.J. McHugh and family. McHugh came west from Ontario in 1873 to work with a survey party. He was a brother of Felix McHugh for whom McHugh Bluff on the north side of Sunnyside is named. At the time of writing this house is in danger of being demolished.

At the intersection of Centre Street and 18th Avenue the street signs list two other names. The NW corner sign shows Centre Street and Volunteer Way. The NE corner sign shows Centre Street and McTavish Street (the former name).

The route continues east on 18th Avenue. Cross 1st Street SE and walk east one more block to Macleod Trail. On the right at this corner is Fire Hall # 2 built in 1912 for joint use by the fire department and the police department although the police only used the building until 1918. Other tenants of the building have been the Royal Canadian Volunteer Reserve and St. John's Ambulance. The Fire Department still uses the building, although there is no firefighting equipment stored here.

From this corner turn left and walk north to 17th Avenue. Cross to the east side of Macleod Trail. Walk north a few steps and use the stairs to access the pedestrian crossing back to the upper level of the station (5.7 km).

Route Summary:

1. From the upper level of the station turn right and cross the pedestrian overpass above Macleod Trail and descend the stairs or ramp to the end of 15th Avenue.
2. Walk west on 15th Avenue to Centre Street.
3. Turn right and walk north to the apartment building at 1411 – Centre Street.
4. Retrace your steps back to 15th Avenue.
5. Turn right and walk west to 1st Street SW.
6. Turn left and walk south one block crossing 17th Avenue into Rouleauville Square.
7. From the south side of the square on 18th Avenue walk one block south on 1st Street to 19th Avenue.

8. Walk west on 19th Avenue to 4th Street.
9. Turn right and walk north one block turning left onto 18th Avenue.
10. Walk west to 5th Street and turn left walking one block south to 19th Avenue.
11. Turn left and walk east on 19th Avenue to 4th Street.
12. Turn right and walk one block south to 20th Avenue.
13. Turn right and walk west to 5th Street.
14. Turn left and walk south to 21st Avenue.
15. Turn left and walk east to 2nd Street.
16. Turn right and walk south to 22nd Avenue.
17. Turn right and walk west to Cliff Street.
18. Turn left and walk south to 23rd Avenue.
19. Turn left and walk east to 2nd Street.
20. Turn right and walk south to 24th Avenue.
21. Turn left and walk east to 1st Street.
22. Turn left and walk north on 1st Street and Holy Cross Lane
23. Turning right onto a path to reach the Lindsay Park west bridge.
24. Cross the bridge and follow the path to the left.
25. At the old train bridge climb some stairs and cross the bridge to the corner of 19th Avenue and 1st Street.
26. Walk north one block and turn right on 18th Avenue.
27. Walk east on 18th Avenue to Macleod Trail.
28. Turn left and walk north to 17th Avenue.
29. Cross to the east side of Macleod Trail.
30. Turn left and climb the stairs on the way back to the station.

Chapter Two
Erlton/Stampede Station

Station Information: The station is on the east side of Macleod Trail just north of 25th Avenue SE. The southwest corner of Stampede Park is on the east side of the station. At the south end of the centre platform the station exit is at ground level. Use caution at 25th Avenue when crossing the tracks. At the north end of the platform, stairs and an escalator lead up to the pedestrian overpass across the northbound track. A second set of stairs and an escalator lead down to ground level. There is no park and ride lot for the station. There is a series of plaques at the upper level of the station with historical information about Canadian National Railway, Macleod Trail, Union Cemetery, Rouleauville and Stampede Park.

The station is named for the community of Erlton established in 1906, west of Macleod Trail and the station. The origin of the name Erlton is unknown. The part of Erlton north of 25th Avenue has undergone extensive changes as most of the older houses have been replaced by townhouses and condos. South of 25th Avenue more of the older homes remain. The former CNR railway yard at the north end of the community has been converted to Lindsay Park, a pleasant inner-city park. Talisman Centre in the park is a very popular fitness and training centre. The area south of the station is often called Cemetery Hill. Five cemeteries are found in close proximity to each other. Overlooking 25th Avenue at the north end of Union Cemetery on the east side of Macleod Trail is Reader Rock Gardens. The gardens were restored after being neglected for a long time.

Erlton/Stampede Walk 1
Reader Rock Gardens & Cemetery Hill

Walk Overview: This loop route starts by wandering through Reader Rock Gardens on the north slope of Cemetery Hill. The route then passes through Union Cemetery and Burnsland Cemetery on the east side of Macleod Trail. A pedestrian overpass across Macleod Trail leads to the Chinese Cemetery. From there you walk past the Jewish Cemetery on the way to St. Mary's Cemetery before returning to the station. A copy of Harry Sanders's book *Calgary's Historic Union Cemetery: A Walking Guide* would be very helpful for this section of the walk.

Length: 4.6 km (This is a minimum distance as you may do some off-route exploring through Reader Rock Gardens or the various cemeteries.)

Route Description & Accessibility: Accessibility on this route is very poor. The route through Reader Rock Gardens up to the top of the hill at the north end of Union Cemetery is on steep trails. There is a descent in Union Cemetery on the way to Burnsland Cemetery followed by an ascent to reach the pedestrian overpass. After visiting St. Mary's Cemetery there is a long steep downhill section on the way back to the station. The walking surface on the route is a mix of sidewalks, trails, cemetery roads and grass. No alternate routes for the ascents/descents are included in the text.

Food and Drink: Reader's Garden Café is open seasonally for lunch on weekdays and for brunch on Saturdays and Sundays from 11 am to 3 pm. You pass a restaurant at Macleod Trail and 25th Avenue.

Washrooms: There are no public washrooms along this route.

Map References: Clear-View – 37 & 36, MapArt – 164
Rand McNally – 60 & 59, Sherlock – 35

Route Category: Walk – The route starts and ends at the station (no bus is required).

The Walk: After getting off the train walk to the south end of the platform by 25th Avenue. Turn right and cross the southbound tracks and walk a few steps to the traffic lights at 25th Avenue and Macleod Trail. Cross to the south side of 25th Avenue and turn left walking across both sets of tracks. Follow a trail angling to the right past the parking lot for Reader Rock Gardens. There are two information plaques about the gardens beside the parking lot. One point of interest is the Entrance Arch near the south end of the parking lot. This sandstone arch built in 1912 is at the base of a set of stairs leading up a slope in the cemetery.

In the mid-1910s Calgary Parks and Cemeteries Superintendent William Reader began designing these rock gardens on a north-facing slope overlooking 25th Avenue SE and Stampede Park. Reader had moved from England to Canada in 1908, becoming a gardener for Pat Burns. In 1913 he became Parks Superintendent, a position he held until 1942. He and his family lived in the Superintendent's Cottage built at the top of the slope on the north side of the cemetery. Most of the garden had been completed by 1930 although Reader continued to collect plants until his death in 1943. He collected over 4,000 different plant species for the garden. After his death the garden was opened to the public and named Reader Rock Garden. The cottage was demolished in 1944. After many years of neglect the gardens became derelict and badly in need of some real care. A federal grant in 2003 made the dream of restoring the gardens possible. As part of the gardens rejuvenation a replica of the original cottage has been constructed. It is used for park educational programs. Today this restored 1.2 hectare garden is a legacy to the dedication of William Reader.

The trail leads past the parking lot to a brick surfaced road leading up the slope to Union Cemetery. As the road turns to the right you turn left through a gateway into the west garden area of Reader Rock Gardens (0.3 km). Use caution on the garden trails as the rocks can be slippery if wet. Within this area there are two constructed pools, flowing water and a small bridge. Continue uphill through the garden on the stone trail to reach an open grass area just to the west of the Cottage. This garden area with a small gazebo, a rather quaint wooden bench, and perennial flowerbeds was a favourite spot for Reader's wife, Rose Martha. This garden was known by the names of The Rose Garden, Rose's garden, Martha's garden or Nana's garden.

To view the High Rockery area of the gardens follow a wider path on the south side of Rose's Garden. The path leads downhill towards the brick road. This slope south of the west garden has a mix of alpine plants, flowering perennials, shrubs and ornamental trees. After viewing this area walk back up the trail towards the cottage. The south slope area separates the area around the cottage from the north fence of Union Cemetery.

Cottage in Reader Rock Garden

Climb up through the south slope area and look for a gateway to enter the north side of the cemetery. Union is Calgary's oldest cemetery still in use. Calgary's first public or Protestant cemetery was established at Shaganappi Point in 1885 near the northeast corner of the present day Shaganappi Golf Course overlooking the Bow River just west of Crowchild Trail. This site proved unsuitable as a cemetery and the town of Calgary purchased 56.5 acres from Augustus Carney, on the hillside south of the exhibition grounds. Close to 75 bodies were then moved to Union Cemetery from Shaganappi in 1892 and the remaining graves were relocated in 1911. It is estimated that between 50,000 and 60,000 graves are now in Union Cemetery.

From the gateway, angle to the right towards the Union Cemetery Mortuary (0.6 km), constructed in 1908 of concrete blocks designed to look like stone. The mortuary was built to deal with the difficulty of trying to dig graves for winter burials. Graveside services could be held upstairs in the chapel and the bodies were then stored in the basement crypt until the ground thawed in the spring. The western slope of Reader Rock Gardens is on the west side of the mortuary. This was the final area of the garden to be developed by Reader.

Union Cemetery Mortuary

From the mortuary continue your exploration of the cemetery. There are two north-south roads in the cemetery. The upper road parallels Macleod Trail along the west side of the cemetery and the lower road parallels Spiller Road along the east side of the cemetery. Numerous roads lead downhill from west to east. Follow one of the roads downhill and turn right along the lower road. At the vehicle entrance road on Spiller Road continue a short distance further south to view Galloway House (1.0 km).

When the cemetery opened in 1890, the original home of the first cemetery caretaker, Augustus Carney, and his wife was located in this general area. Carney and his wife lived in their house until 1892. Robert Barker was the second cemetery caretaker from 1892 until 1899. At that time the former Carney home was demolished and replaced by the Galloway House. James Galloway became the cemetery caretaker in 1899. The house is presently used as office space for the foreman and cemetery staff.

Prior to the building of Victoria Road on the west side of Union Cemetery in 1912, the present-day Spiller Road served as a main road leading into Calgary from the south. The route passed through the Ramsay community on the way to downtown. On Victoria Park/Stampede Walk 2 – Ramsay and Scotchman's Hill you will pass two older sidewalks stamps in the community that still show the Macleod Trail name. Later the road on the west side of Union cemetery was renamed Macleod Trail. Macleod Trail is named for Colonel James Macleod. He became a NWMP commissioner in 1876 and the following year he negotiated Treaty No. 7 with the five First Nations groups living in Southern Alberta. He became a magistrate and judge for the North-West Territories in 1880. Colonel Macleod School in Renfrew is named in his honour. Spiller Road is named for Edward "Ted" Spiller. He was a long time volunteer with the Boy Scouts.

From Galloway House retrace your steps back to the entrance road on Spiller Road. Use caution crossing to the east side of Spiller Road to Burnsland Cemetery. There is no crosswalk but the traffic is usually fairly light. Burnsland Cemetery with about 22,000 graves opened in 1923. From Spiller Road, walk east along Cemetery Road, a gravel road on the north side of Burnsland Cemetery. Cemetery Road reaches a junction at a gateway. Two roads lead southeast and southwest into the cemetery from the gateway. Follow the left branch. The two branches join later forming a diamond shape.

The left branch leads to the Field of Honour where many of the city's war veterans are buried. The many crosses in the Field of Honour serve as a somber reminder of how many individuals fought and died in the war. In the Field of Honour is the Cross of Sacrifice, one of 26 such crosses in Canada (1.5 km).

Military section in Burnsland Cemetery

After reaching the south junction of the two roads turn right and follow the other road back to the north fence. Walk west along Cemetery Road and cross back over Spiller Road into Union Cemetery. Select a different east-west road from the earlier route and walk back uphill across the cemetery to the west side road overlooking Macleod Trail. Turn left and follow this road south to the pedestrian overpass above Macleod Trail (2.9 km).

The overpass ramp on the west side of Macleod Trail is beside 31st Avenue at the north end of the Chinese Cemetery. This small 1.4 hectare cemetery, established in 1908, has over 1,000 graves of Calgary's Chinese pioneers. The Calgary Chinese Memorial Monument near the entrance describes the many hardships endured by these pioneers when they moved to Canada in the 1880s seeking employment. Many of the workers died during the construction of the CPR through the mountains of Alberta and British Columbia. In 1980, during the construction of the LRT tunnel south of Erlton Station and the widening of Macleod Trail, thirty-nine bodies were unearthed near the cemetery. The Te Hoy Sun Association chose to bury these bodies in a common grave marked with one monument.

From 31st Avenue walk north along the alley on the west side of the Shaw building to reach the Jewish Cemetery on the north side of 30th Avenue (3.2 km). This 1.3 hectare cemetery, established in 1904, has about 2,300 graves. The cemetery includes a war memorial (veterans' cenotaph), an infants' memorial and a prayer book depository (genizah). There is a locked security gate so you will only be able to view the cemetery by walking west outside the fence on 30th Avenue along the south side of the cemetery.

Continue west along 30th Avenue and turn left on Erlton Street. One block south on the right is the entrance to St. Mary's Cemetery with its sandstone gateposts (3.4 km). Calgary's first Roman Catholic cemetery was established in 1876 near 2nd Street and 23rd Avenue SW. The city took over the management of the cemetery in 1935 and moved it to this 7.1 hectares site on both sides of Erlton Street. At that time the graves in the Mission district were exhumed and moved to this cemetery. Today there are over 15,000 graves in the cemetery. Just to the right near the entrance are the graves of Bishop Carroll and Bishop O'Byrne. Nearby are the graves of numerous priests. Further north in the cemetery is an area with nuns' graves.

Wooden crosses in St. Mary's Cemetery

From St. Mary's Cemetery entrance turn left and walk north on Erlton Street going down a steep hill to 25th Avenue. Turn right and walk east to Macleod Trail. Cross to the northeast corner and retrace the first part of the walk back to the station (4.6 km).

Route Summary:

1. After getting off the train walk to the south end of the platform at 25th Avenue.
2. Turn right and cross the tracks walking a few steps west to the traffic lights at 25th Avenue and Macleod Trail.
3. Cross to the south side of 25th Avenue and turn left crossing both sets of tracks.
4. Angle to the right on a trail that passes the Reader Rock Gardens parking lot.
5. The trail ends at a brick surfaced road leading up the slope to Union Cemetery.
6. As the road turns right, turn left through a gateway into the west garden area of Reader Rock Gardens.
7. Continue uphill through the garden to the grass area just west of the cottage.
8. To view the High Rockery area follow a wider path downhill from the grass area.
9. Retrace your steps and climb up the south slope overlooking the cottage.
10. Look for a gateway in the fence on the north side of the cemetery.
11. Angle to the right to the Union Cemetery Mortuary.
12. From the mortuary choose one of the east-west roads leading downhill to the Spiller Road side of the cemetery.
13. Walk south along the road on the Spiller Road side of the cemetery to view Galloway House.
14. Retrace your steps back to the east entrance to the cemetery and cross to the east side of Spiller Road near the northwest corner of Burnsland Cemetery.
15. Walk east along Cemetery Road to a gateway in the north fence.
16. Enter the cemetery and take the road leading to the left. This road and the right road meet further south.
17. After reaching the south junction of the two roads turn right and follow the other road back to the north fence.
18. Walk back along Cemetery Road to Spiller Road, cross the road and go back into Union Cemetery.
19. Pick a different east-west road and walk uphill to the north-south road on the west side of the cemetery beside Macleod Trail.
20. Turn left and follow the road south to a pedestrian overpass.

21. Cross the overpass to the west side of Macleod Trail.
22. The Chinese Cemetery is south of the west end of the overpass.
23. From 31st Avenue by the overpass follow a back alley north to 30th Avenue on the south side of the Jewish Cemetery.
24. Walk west along 30th Avenue and turn left on Erlton Street.
25. At 31st Avenue turn right into St. Mary's Cemetery.
26. From the cemetery entrance turn left and head north on Erlton Street going down a steep hill to 25th Avenue.
27. Turn right and follow 25th Avenue back to Macleod Trail.
28. Cross to the northeast corner of the intersection and return to the station.

Erlton/Stampede Walk 2
Cliff Bungalow

Walk Overview: This route heads west from Macleod Trail on 25th Avenue crossing Scollen Bridge and continuing west to 5th Street SW. The route then makes a small loop through the north end of Elbow Park climbing up onto the top of the escarpment on the south side of Mount Royal. After descending the escarpment the route makes a loop through Cliff Bungalow along Cliff Street and 5th Street before returning to the station. Cliff Bungalow-Mission Community is made up of two adjacent communities that operate as one community association. The area of both communities was annexed by the city in 1907 and then developed in the early part of the 20th century. Cliff Bungalow is bounded on the north by 17th Avenue, on the east by 4th Street, on the west by 5A St and Cliff Street and on the south by the Elbow River. The land in this area became CPR property in 1882. In 1907 the area between 4th and 5th Streets was subdivided and given the name "addition to the city of Calgary". Three years later the land between 5th Street and the escarpment (cliff) was added and called "an extension of Mount Royal". Later the area was called Cliff Bungalow after the bungalow school on Cliff Street. On the walk you will see blue street signs showing both the current street number and the historic name.

Length: 6.2 km

Route Description & Accessibility: The ascent/descent on the escarpment is very steep with poor accessibility. An alternate route that avoids this section is included in the text. The area near the intersection of 25th Avenue and Cliff Street has a short ascent/descent. Most of the remainder of the route is very flat with good accessibility. The surface for most of the route is on sidewalks.

Food and Drink: At the south end of 4th Street you are close to several restaurants, coffee shops and a grocery store.

Washrooms: There are no public washrooms along this route.

Map References: Clear-View – 36, MapArt – 164
Rand McNally – 59, Sherlock – 35 & 27

Route Category: Walk – The route starts and ends at the station (no bus is required).

The Walk: Walk to the south end of the station platform and turn right at 25th Avenue. Cross the tracks and walk a few steps to the traffic lights at Macleod Trail and 25th Avenue. Cross to the west side of Macleod Trail and continue westbound on 25th Avenue crossing Scollen Bridge (0.4 km). The former 25th Avenue Bridge was renamed Scollen Bridge in recognition of Father Constantine Scollen for whom 25th Avenue was originally named. Scollen played an important role as an interpreter and intermediary for the First Nations during the signing of Treaties 6 and 7. This section of the route from the station to the bridge is the same as Walk 3 in this chapter.

After crossing the bridge continue west along 25th Avenue. You pass the Avonlea Apartments building at 208 – 25th Avenue. This two-storey brick building constructed in 1914 is one of nine pre-WWI apartments in the Mission community. Further west on this block is the Hickey Residence at 231 – 25th Avenue. A. Francis Hickey, the manager of Calgary Typesetting Co., and members of his family lived here from 1912 to 1949. In the 1970s the building was converted into suites. Today, the building is surrounded by high-rise condos.

The route continues west along 25th Avenue crossing 4th Street. In the block between 4th and 5th Streets is an interesting building. The Himmelman Boathouse building was constructed in 1926, by a boat builder from Nova Scotia, Arthur Himmelman. He became a member of the Calgary Yacht Club and started building boats for members of the club. He also built the Gordon Suites in 1929 adjacent to the boathouse and the Laurence Apartments in 1930 at 2400 – 5th Street SW. These two buildings are named after his sons. Gordon Himmelman operated a woodcraft business in the boathouse after his father's death in 1947. Laurence Himmelman then operated a construction business in the boathouse until he sold the building in 2004. The Gordon Suites are two mirror-image side-by-side apartment buildings.

At 5th Street the route crosses to the west side of the intersection and turns left (1.1 km). Walking south towards Elbow Drive you pass the Aberhart Residence at 2505 – 5th Street. This house, constructed in 1925, was the former home of Alberta premier William Aberhart. He was a high school principal and a well-known lay preacher broadcasting his "Back to the Bible Hour" program on Sundays. In 1927 Aberhart also established the Prophetic Bible Institute located in the 500 block of 8th Avenue SW. One of the boarders in Aberhart's home was a young Ernest Manning who later succeeded Aberhart as premier.

Turn right at the next corner and head in a southwesterly direction along Elbow Drive. In a short distance you reach Garden Crescent, a cul-de-sac on the right (1.4 km). In 1911 the 9-metre-wide and 76-metre-long median on this street was planted with trees, shrubs and perennials. There are 15 houses around the edge of the median. Garden Crescent is named for James Hay Garden, a builder who was elected for three terms as an alderman between 1910 and 1923. In 1915 he was elected City commissioner. For many years Garden was on the board of governors at Mount Royal College. The uniqueness of this street is recognized as an historic resource.

After viewing Garden Crescent retrace your steps to Elbow Drive, turn right and continue to the next corner at 25th Avenue. Turn right and head west. On the left near Glencoe Road there are several older sandstone homes. On the north side of 25th Avenue is the Glencoe Club, established in 1931. At 25th Avenue and 7th Street (2.1 km) follow a paved path leading up the south-facing escarpment on the north side of the Glencoe Club. If you require better accessibility than this steep path retrace your steps back to 5th Street and 25th Avenue. From here turn left up a short incline to the end

Garden Crescent

of 25th Avenue. Hillcrest Avenue is on the left and Cliff Street is on the right. At this point you rejoin the walk route.

At the top of the slope turn right and follow a trail east along the top of the escarpment to where it meets Earl Grey Crescent (2.4 km). Continue east along the south side of Earl Grey Crescent passing a set of stairs that leads down to the Glencoe Club parking lot. Earl Grey Crescent turns left and heads north to join Hillcrest Avenue just east of 7th Street.

Turn right and follow Hillcrest Avenue down the slope into the community of Cliff Bungalow. At the bottom of the slope is a three-way intersection (3.1 km). On your right is 25th Avenue and straight ahead is Cliff Street. On the southeast corner of the intersection is the Millican Residence (Twin Gables), a two-storey wood frame house built in 1913-14. The building is named for the twin gables on the north side above the main entrance. The home's first resident was Albert Millican, who partnered a law firm with his brother William. In 1931 a foreclosure on the property forced the family to move. William Millican developed the Millican Estates community north of the community of Ogden. Businessman Wellington Walker moved into the house in 1932. Today the house is privately operated as a bed and breakfast. Note the two lion heads on either side of the east door.

From this corner, head north along Cliff Street past a community park. On the left there are a few homes before you reach the treed escarpment slope. Restoration work has been taking place on the slope. The route passes the Cliff Bungalow School building constructed in 1920. Several bungalow schools were built to accommodate the increasing number of students. This building is identical in design to Tuxedo School. The building's tenants are the Mission Cliff Bungalow Community Association and a Montessori School. Other examples of bungalow school buildings still standing are Riverside and Balmoral. Across the road from the school on the southeast corner is the Somerville Duplex, a two-storey brick building constructed by Herbert Rowan in 1912 for businessman William Somerville. At the time of writing the building is undergoing extensive renovations.

Continue walking north on Cliff Street towards Royal Avenue. On the southwest corner of Royal Avenue and Cliff Street is the Holy Angels School building (3.6 km). The north end of the bungalow school was constructed in 1919 with the addition on the south end being added in 1929. The building is very similar in design to St. John's School on Kensington Road. Note the use of the lion heads to hold the chains that support the canopy over the front entrance.

From the intersection at Royal Avenue jog slightly to the right and continue north on 5A Street. The blue street sign indicates that 5A Street

Cliff Bungalow School

was called University Street. The College Apartments are at 1722 – 5A Street. This two-storey brick building now called the Carolina Apartments was built in 1911 at a time when there were only 25 apartment buildings in the city. The land on which the building was constructed was formerly owned by Western Canada College, the predecessor of Western Canada High School. One of the early owners of the Carolina Apartments was Frank Fairey who built Fairey Terrace at 12th Avenue and 3rd Street SE.

Continue north on 5A Street and turn left on 17th Avenue, formerly called Notre Dame Avenue. Walk west to the front of Western Canada High School (4.1 km). The school building has had several additions since the school opened in 1929. The school is built on part of the 8.1 hectares site of the former Western Canada College. The present high school site is 4.5 hectares. On the front lawn of the school facing towards the intersection of 17th Avenue and 6th Street is a cenotaph commemorating the students of Western Canada College who died in World War 1.

From the front of the school retrace your steps back to 5A Street and continue east one more block to 5th Street and turn right. The street sign indicates that 5th Street used to be called College Street. Heading south on 5th Street, you will pass more blue signs indicating the former street names. The names of the avenues were English-based names in Cliff Bungalow and French-based names on the east side of 4th Street in Mission. It is interesting that the names of former governor-generals of Canada were used in these original street names for Cliff Bungalow.

Grey Avenue (now 18th Avenue) was named for Albert Henry Grey, 4th Earl Grey, 9th Governor General of Canada. He supported football and donated the Grey Cup to the champions of Senior Amateur Football. Minto Avenue (now 19th Avenue) was named for Gilbert Elliot-Murray-Kynynmound, 4th Earl of Minto, 8th Governor General of Canada who donated the Minto Cup in 1901 to be awarded to the champion senior men's lacrosse team in Canada. The cup has been awarded to the junior men's champions since 1937.

Aberdeen Avenue (now 20th Avenue) was named for John Hamilton-Gordon, 1st Marquis of Aberdeen and Temair, 7th Governor General of Canada. Stanley Avenue (now 21st Avenue) was named for Frederick Arthur Stanley, 16th Earl of Derby, 6th Governor General of Canada. In 1892 he donated the Stanley Cup trophy as a challenge cup for Canada's best amateur hockey club. Since 1909, only professional teams have competed for the Stanley Cup.

Lansdowne Avenue (now 22nd Avenue) was named for Henry Petty-Fitzmaurice, 5th Marquis of Lansdowne, 5th Governor General of Canada. Lorne Avenue (now 23rd Avenue) was named for John George Campbell, 9th Duke of Argyll, but better known as the Marquis of Lorne. He was the 4th Governor General of Canada. His name is now used for the Marquis of Lorne Trail (Highway 22X) at the south end of the city.

Dufferin Street (now 24th Avenue) was named for Frederick Hamilton-Temple-Blackwood, 1st Marquess of Dufferin, 3rd Governor General of Canada. Monck Street (now 25th Avenue) was named for Charles Stanley Monck, 4th Viscount Monck. He was the last Governor General of the Province of Canada and after Confederation the first Governor General of Canada.

It is interesting to note that eight of Canada's first nine Governor Generals after Confederation had streets named after them. The exception was the second Governor General, John Young, 1st Baron Lisgar, whose name was not included in the naming of these streets. Several streets in Mount Royal community (Dorchester, Colborne, Durham, Sydenham and Bagot) are named after Governor Generals who served prior to Confederation in 1867.

On 5th Street you pass the Treend House built in 1922 at 1933 – 5th Street as a retirement home for rancher William Treend. Further south on 5th Street you pass the Yale Apartments at 2121 – 5th Street. This building was constructed in 1910 as a single-family home but is now used as an apartment building. You then pass the 24th Avenue Cottage School, also known as Beverly Apartments at 2300 – 5th Street. This school opened in 1911 but only served as a school for 17 years. The building was converted into four suites in 1928 and renamed Beverly Apartments in 1931. In 1935 the Calgary School District was operating eighteen two-room cottage schools and seventeen four-room schools. Very few of these buildings remain today. Continue south on 5th Street to 25th Avenue (5.1 km). Turn left and retrace your steps east along 25th Avenue back to the station (6.2 km).

Route Summary:

1. Walk south to the end of the platform at 25th Avenue and turn right.
2. Cross the southbound tracks and walk a few steps to the traffic lights at Macleod Trail.
3. Cross to the west side of Macleod Trail and continue westbound on 25th Avenue crossing Scollen Bridge.
4. After the bridge continue westbound on 25th Avenue to 4th Street.
5. Cross 4th Street and continue one block to 5th Street.
6. Cross to the west side of 5th Street and turn left walking south one block to Elbow Drive.
7. Turn right along Elbow Drive.
8. Turn right onto Garden Crescent and walk to the end of the cul-de-sac.
9. Retrace your steps back to Elbow Drive and turn right. Continue to the next corner where 25th Avenue meets Elbow Drive.
10. Turn right on 25th Avenue and walk west to 7th Street.
11. Turn right and follow a paved path up the escarpment slope on the north side of the Glencoe Club.
12. Turn right and walk along the top of the escarpment.
13. At Earl Grey Crescent continue beside the road along the top of the escarpment.
14. When Earl Grey Crescent meets Hillcrest Avenue turn right and follow Hillcrest down the hill to where it meets 25th Avenue on the right and Cliff Street on the left.
15. Turn left and follow Cliff Street north to Royal Avenue.
16. Angle slightly to the right and follow 5A Street north to 17th Avenue.
17. Turn left and walk west to the front of Western Canada High School at 6th Street.
18. Retrace your steps back to 5A Street and walk one more block east on 17th Avenue to 5th Street.
19. Turn right on 5th Street and walk south to 25th Avenue.
20. Turn left and retrace your route back along 25th Avenue to the station.

Erlton/Stampede Walk 3
Rideau Park & Roxboro

Walk Overview: The route heads west on 25th Avenue to Scollen Bridge. From there follow the Elbow River Pathway to J.H. Woods Park. The middle part of the route wanders along tree-lined streets in the older communities of Rideau Park (pre 1920) and Roxboro (1920s). Rideau Park is likely named for the Rideau River and Canal in Ottawa. Developer Fred Lowes introduced the name Roxborough Place in 1912. In Scotland there is a town called Roxburgh. The two communities are a mix of older single-family homes with some new houses being added in the past few years. Near the end of the walk the route passes through Lindsay Park.

Length: 5.4 km

Route Description & Accessibility: Most of this route has very good accessibility. The most challenging areas are a wooden surfaced pedestrian bridge connecting J.H. Woods Park to Rideau Park community and a trail beside the river at the north end of Roxboro Park.

Food and Drink: There are picnic tables and/or benches in Lindsay Park and in J.H. Woods Park. The route passes close to a grocery store, several restaurants and coffee shops near 4th Street and 26th Avenue.

Washrooms: There are washrooms in the Talisman Sports Centre in Lindsay Park.

Map References: Clear-View – 36, MapArt – 164
Rand McNally – 59, Sherlock – 35

Route Category: Walk – The route starts and ends at the station (no bus is required).

The Walk: Walk south on the station platform to 25th Avenue and turn right. Cross the tracks and walk a few steps to the traffic lights at Macleod Trail and 25th Avenue.

Cross to the southwest corner of Macleod Trail and 25th Avenue. Continue westbound along 25th Avenue crossing Scollen Bridge (0.4 km) and turning immediately left onto a path leading south beside the river. The path ends when you reach 26th Avenue. There are a few steps on the road to reach the sidewalk in front of Elbow Towers (a high-rise apartment building on the left). Continue west on 26th Avenue past 1st Street (formerly Jean Baptiste Street).

From 2nd to 4th Street, you walk along the Elbow River Promenade on the south side of 26th Avenue. Several information plaques describe the history of Mission and Cliff Bungalow communities. Victoria Park/Stampede Walk 3 – Mission 2nd and 4th Streets also visits the Elbow River Promenade.

At 4th Street is Mission Bridge, Calgary's oldest concrete bridge (1.1 km). Cross to the west side of 4th Street at the north end of the bridge. Elbow Drive starts on the west side of 4th Street. Before setting off along the path beside Elbow Drive take a few minutes to explore Elbow Islands Park. Access to the park is by a set of stairs about halfway across the bridge on the west side of 4th Street. In 1975 this small island area below the bridge was donated to the City of Calgary by Canadian Pacific Railway subsidiary, Marathon Realty Company Limited, in recognition of Calgary's Centennial and the railway's historical association with the city. The island's walking trail amongst the dense shrubs and trees can become very overgrown and muddy. When the Elbow River is running high, it would be wise not to venture down the stairs into the park.

Retrace your steps back to the north side of the bridge and turn left following the path beside Elbow Drive. This first section of path might be considered an extension of J. H. Woods Park. The path is right beside Elbow Drive with trees and shrubs on your left separating you from the river. Although the traffic noise on Elbow Drive can be a bit distracting the scenic view of the river provides a positive balance. Near 29th Avenue the green space beside the river widens and the path splits as you enter the main area of J. H. Woods Park. Follow the left path closer to the river.

J. H. Woods Park is a long thin park sandwiched between Elbow Drive on the west and the Elbow River on the east. In the 1920s Colonel James H. Woods, the publisher of the Calgary Herald from 1907 to 1935, donated this land for use as a park. The park was first named Elbow Boulevard Park but after Colonel Woods died in 1941 the park was renamed in his honour. Woods was also very involved with the Boy Scouts. Camp Woods at Sylvan Lake was named in his honour. The Woods Foundation was created from his estate. Funding from the foundation was donated to assist with the establishment of Heritage Park and the building of the aviary conservatory at the Calgary Zoo.

The first point of historical significance in the park was the Elbow Park Swimming Hole and Grounds established on this site in 1914 as the first public swimming facility in Calgary. The small dressing room building in the park was added in 1922 (1.7 km). For many years this location was almost as popular as Bowness Park. In the winter, this section of the Elbow River was used for skating.

On the south side of the building is a playground. The sculpture *The Oarsman* by Robert Spaith which honours John MacMillan Sterling Lecky (1940-2003) is nearby. The sculpture recognizes Lecky's accomplishments as an athlete, entrepreneur, philanthropist and adventurer. A few steps beyond the sculpture you enter a more formal area of the park with a trail

The dressing room building constructed in 1922 in J.H. Woods Park

passing between the hedges arranged in a formal pattern. Look for a plaque in this area recognizing Freddie Lowes, a prominent early Calgary developer in the communities of Elbow Park, Rideau Park and Roxboro. His former home shown on the next page was located on this site.

Continuing a few steps south from the hedges you reach Gerry Shaw Gardens dedicated to Gerry Shaw (1942-1995). A native Calgarian, Shaw played football for the Calgary Stampeders and then became a successful businessman. Family and friends organized the Friends of Gerry Shaw Committee and raised the funds for the development of this park.

Walking a little further south in the park, you reach a pedestrian footbridge crossing the river to the Rideau Park community (2.0 km). The bridge is also on the route for 39th Avenue Walk 1 – Parkhill & Elbow Park. This older pedestrian bridge is one of three similar bridges spanning the Elbow River. The second bridge is on Sifton Boulevard at 8th Street across from Elbow Park School and the third bridge is in Sandy Beach Park. A similar bridge crosses the north channel of the Bow River at the Calgary Zoo.

F.C. Lowes Residence, 1911. Glenbow Archives NA-3918-11

Calgary Greenhouses, ca. 1911. Glenbow Archives NC-24-147

After crossing the bridge turn left. At the first corner on 31st Avenue look right to view Rideau Park School, built in 1930. The old sidewalk stamp on the southeast corner is spelled Riderau Road. Continue one more block on Rideau Road and turn right onto 30th Avenue. This first block is close to the site of the Whitburn Greenhouses shown in the photo on the previous page. At the top of the hill in the photo is the original Earl Grey School on Earl Grey Crescent. Turn left on 5A Street and walk one short block back to Rideau Road and turn right. The 10th Calgary Troop Scout Hall (Sara Scout Hall) is on your right at 609 Rideau Road. The hall, built in 1927, is the oldest scout hall in Calgary. The 10th Scout Troop was established in 1914, meeting first in the Elbow View Hotel at 338 – 26th Avenue and then at the Albion Hotel. A fire destroyed that building in 1925 and the troop was left without a place to meet. Frederick Leslie Sara was the troop's leader from 1923 to 1934. Sara's dedication helped in the building of the troop's own hall in 1927 on land that was donated. In 1948 a ceremony was held to rename the hall in honour of the troop's former leader. Another old sidewalk stamp dated 1913 is on the southeast corner of 5th Street and Rideau Road.

Sara Scout Hall on Rideau Road

Continue east on Rideau Road and cross 4th Street (2.7 km). The street name changes from Rideau Road to Roxboro Road as you leave Rideau Park and enter Roxboro. Walk one block east on Roxboro Road and turn right at 3rd Street. Walk one block south and turn left onto 30th Avenue. On the southwest corners of 2nd Street and 1st Street the sidewalk stamps are dated 1912. On the northwest corner at Roxboro Glen Road and 30th Avenue there used to be a sidewalk stamp indicating that Roxboro Glen Road was once called Centre Street.

Cross Roxboro Glen Road into Roxboro Park (3.4 km). At the south end of the park the tennis courts are named in honour of Derek Lester. A small building south of the tennis courts is named Marion Gibson Hall. From the south end of the park, wander through the park to where the north end fronts on the Elbow River. In the park you pass a plaque on a large rock honouring Bill Milne. Milne played an important role in Calgary as an architect and an environmentalist. He was a strong supporter for the idea of developing a pathway system in Calgary.

A dirt trail leads from the intersection of Roxboro Road and Roxboro Glen Road to the northeast corner of the park. A few steps south of this location a trail leads up the Erlton Roxboro Natural Area escarpment slope on the east side of the park. At the top of the slope is the west side of St. Mary's Cemetery. The cemetery is on the route for Erlton/Stampede Walk 1 – Reader Rock Gardens and Cemetery Hill. From the northeast corner of Roxboro Park follow a trail between the houses on the right and the Elbow River on the left. The trail leads to Forrest Park, a small green park between houses. Walk through the park to reach Erlton Street. A small plaque in the park dated 1997 recognizes the donation of the land for the park by Frances Forrest-Richards MD in memory of Ann Elizabeth and James Forrest.

Turn left and walk north on Erlton Street to 25th Avenue. Turn left and walk through Erlton Park, a small park on the corner, and follow the path under Scollen Bridge (4.0 km). Follow the path downstream to Lindsay Park. A large information sign with a map at the southwest corner of the park provides information about the Elbow River Pathway. When the path divides at the south side of Lindsay Park, take the right branch and enter the main doors of Talisman Centre (4.5 km). Lindsay Park is named after Dr. Neville James Lindsay who came to Calgary in the 1880s. He became involved in real estate after retiring from his medical practice. Lindsay also served as a town and city alderman. On 39th Avenue Station Walk 1 – Parkhill & Elbow Park the route passes by Lindsay's Folly on Heritage Escarpment slope between Rideau Park and Parkhill. On that site Dr. Lindsay had plans to build a home on the escarpment slope but it was never finished.

Walk through Talisman Centre and exit by the north doors. The centre has washrooms and a small snack bar. Outside the north doors, angle to the right to reach the Elbow River Pathway on the north side of the park. Turn right and follow the path under Pattison Bridge at 1st Street, Victoria Bridge at Macleod Trail and the LRT Bridge. Pattison Bridge is named for Private John George Pattison (1875-1917), the only Calgary resident to receive the Victoria Cross in WWI. In 1944 Ian Bazalgette was posthumously awarded the Victoria Cross. He was the only native-born Calgarian awarded the Victoria Cross. A school in Forest Lawn is named in his honour.

After going under the third bridge turn right and follow the sidewalk to the station entrance. Two sets of stairs and an escalator lead up to the upper level of the station where the historical plaques are located. Stairs lead down to the station platform (5.4 km).

Route Summary:
1. Walk to the south end of the platform at 25th Avenue and turn right.
2. Cross the southbound tracks and walk a few steps to the traffic lights at Macleod Trail.
3. Cross to the west side of Macleod Trail and continue westbound on 25th Avenue crossing Scollen Bridge.
4. On the west side of the bridge turn left and follow a path south to 26th Avenue to where the path ends.
5. Walk a few steps west on the road to reach the sidewalk in front of Elbow Towers.
6. Continue west on 26th Avenue to 4th Street SW.
7. Cross to the west side of 4th Street and walk a few steps south on Mission Bridge to a set of stairs leading down to Elbow Islands Park.
8. After exploring the park climb the stairs and walk back to the north end of the bridge.
9. Turn left and head west along the south side of Elbow Drive.
10. When the path splits near 29th Avenue and Elbow Drive take the left branch.
11. Follow a trail through an ornamental area with hedges and walk a few more steps to reach Gerry Shaw Park.
12. Walk a little further south in the park and turn left onto a pedestrian bridge over the river.
13. On the far side of the bridge turn left on Rideau Road.
14. Walk a few steps on Rideau Road and turn right on 30th Avenue.
15. Follow 30th Avenue east and turn left on 5A Street.
16. Walk one block north and turn right on Rideau Road.
17. Continue east on Rideau Road and cross to the east side of 4th Street.
18. Walk one block east on Roxboro Road and turn right on 3rd Street.
19. Walk one block south and turn left on 30th Avenue.
20. Walk east and cross Roxboro Glen Road into Roxboro Park.

21. Walk north through the park to Roxboro Road.
22. Follow a trail angling to the northeast corner of the park beside the Elbow River.
23. Follow the trail along the riverbank and turn right into a small park between houses to reach Erlton Street.
24. Walk through the park to Erlton Street.
25. Turn left and walk north to 25th Avenue.
26. Turn left and cross through Erlton Park following a path under Scollen Bridge to the north side of 25th Avenue.
27. Follow the path north to Lindsay Park.
28. When the path divides take the right branch and enter the front doors of Talisman Centre.
29. Walk through the Centre and exit by the north doors.
30. Angle to the right and follow a path down a small slope to reach the Elbow River Pathway on the north side of the park.
31. Turn right and follow the path east under Pattison Bridge, Victoria Bridge and the LRT Bridge.
32. After the third bridge turn right and follow the sidewalk back to the station.

Chapter Three
39th Avenue Station

Station Information: The station is located at the intersection of 39th Avenue and Burnsland Road SE in a light industrial area known as Manchester Industrial North. Macleod Trail is one block west of the station. The station has side platforms that you exit at ground level. Use caution when crossing the tracks at the north end of the platforms. There is a park and ride lot beside the station. West across Macleod Trail is the community of Parkhill situated on land annexed by the city in 1910. The west side of Parkhill is on top of Heritage Escarpment overlooking the Elbow River. Picturesque Stanley Park is at the south end of Parkhill beside the Elbow River.

West across the Elbow River from Parkhill is the community of Elbow Park. James Morris had a homestead in the area that is now the 900 block of Sifton Boulevard. James Owens homesteaded in the area that is now east of Elbow Drive. In 1887 he built a racetrack and stables. William Scollen was homesteading in the Glencoe area along Elbow Drive. In the area near present day Riverdale and Lansdowne Avenues, James Butlin had a homestead.

By 1906, the owners of the land that became the community of Elbow Park were Colin George Ross and Felix McHugh. Developer Freddie Lowes became involved in the selling of lots starting in 1907. One of Lowes' more creative ideas was his use of a hydraulic pump to wash dirt from the slope of Mission Hill. The dirt was used as fill in a swampy area where Roxboro community was then developed. From 1911 to 1915 houses were being constructed in the area known as Glencoe (along Elbow Drive), Garden Crescent and East Elbow Park.

39th Avenue Walk 1
Parkhill & Elbow Park

Walk Overview: This route combines an out-and-back section with a loop through the communities of Parkhill, Elbow Park and Rideau Park. The route descends the Heritage Escarpment slope at the south end of Rideau Park and crosses the Elbow River. After wandering through Elbow Park on both sides of Elbow Drive the route climbs the escarpment slope and wanders through Parkhill before returning to the station. Points of interest include the Southern Alberta Pioneers Building, Princess Obolensky Park, several historic buildings and an interesting mix of older and new homes.

Length: 8.9 km

Route Description & Accessibility: The steep Heritage Escarpment slope has poor accessibility. No alternate route to avoid this slope is included in the text. The portion of the route in Elbow Park is relatively flat with good accessibility. The walking surface along the route is a mix of sidewalks, paved paths and dirt trails.

Food and Drink: There are benches and/or tables in Elbow Park Community Park and in J.H. Woods Park.

Washrooms: Stanley Park has seasonal public washrooms.

Map References: Clear-View – 36, MapArt – 164
Rand McNally – 59, Sherlock – 35

Route Category: Walk – The route starts and ends at the station (no bus is required).

The Walk: From the north end of the station platform turn left on 39th Avenue and walk west one block to Macleod Trail. Cross Macleod Trail and continue west on 39th Avenue on a short ascent to Stanley Road on the east side of the Parkhill/Stanley Park Community Association Park.

Turn right on Stanley Road and then left on 38A Avenue. One long block west on 38A Avenue will take you to 1A Street SW. Cross to the west side of 1A Street to the top of Heritage Escarpment overlooking the Elbow River and the eastern part of Elbow Park across the river.

Follow the dirt trail to the right along the top of the escarpment. In a couple of blocks the route reaches the small ornamental Princess Obolensky Park at the south end of 4th Street (0.9 km). She was born in the principality of Obolensk in Central Russia, moving to Calgary in 1931. She became the proprietor of Calgary's first clothing boutique. After her death in 1984, the park was dedicated through the efforts of her friends and the Calgary Beautification Foundation.

From the park continue a few steps further along the top of the escarpment and turn right, walking a short distance north on 4th Street to the entrance gate for the Southern Alberta Pioneers and Descendants Association building. The names of early Southern Alberta pioneers and the individuals present at the signing of Treaty Seven are listed on plaques on the gateposts. Members of the association have to be direct descendants of someone who, prior to 1891, was living in the area that became Southern Alberta.

Small bridge on the path below Lindsay's Folly

Walk a few steps further north from the gate and follow the paved path to the left across the park on the north side of the pioneers' building. Shortly after the path starts down the escarpment there is a junction. Take the left branch walking past a few brick remains in the area known as Lindsay's Folly. This is the location where Dr. Neville Lindsay started to build a large brick and sandstone home in 1913. Dr. Lindsay never completed the home. Lindsay Park, where Talisman Centre is located was named for Dr. Lindsay. Further down the escarpment the path crosses an old cement bridge.

At the bottom of the escarpment turn right on the Elbow River Pathway. It is a short walk to the south end of Rideau Road. Walk north on Rideau Road. At 32nd Avenue (a very short section of road) turn right and then turn left along an unnamed road/alley in front of Rideau Park School (1.8 km). The school was built in 1930 on a 1.4 hectare site. The escarpment to the east of the school was used as a buffalo jump with skulls of these animals being discovered during the excavation for the school. Prior to the school being built, William Whitburn pastured his dairy cattle on the land where the school was built. Whitburn's greenhouse business was located just north of the school along 30th Avenue. Erlton/Stampede Walk 3 – Rideau Park &

Roxboro goes along 30th Avenue past the former greenhouse site. From the front of the school follow 31st Avenue back to Rideau Road and turn left. Walk a short distance south and turn right, crossing the pedestrian bridge over the Elbow River. Erlton/Stampede Walk 3 – Rideau Park and Roxboro also crosses this bridge. There are two similar bridges upstream at Sifton Boulevard near 8th Street and in Sandy Beach.

On the far side of the bridge is J.H. Woods Park. Colonel Woods donated the land for park use in the 1920s. After Woods' death in 1941, the original name of Elbow Boulevard Park was changed to J.H. Woods Park. Continue straight ahead from the bridge and use the pedestrian crossing light to reach the west side of Elbow Drive.

Continue straight ahead in a westerly direction on 32nd Avenue to the northeast corner of Elbow Park Community Park at 7th Street (2.2 km). Turn left and walk south along the edge of the park to 34th Avenue and make a right turn. There are several points of interest as you walk west along 34th Avenue towards a heavily treed escarpment slope on the west side of 8th Street. On the southeast corner of 7A Street is the former AGT South Exchange building constructed in 1928. When the larger substation was built on the southwest corner the older building was sold and is now a private residence. On the right on the north side of 34th Avenue are the community hall and some private tennis courts. A plaque in front of the hall honours members of nearby Christ Church Anglican who lost their lives in WWI. Note the bike rack with a sign advertising The Star Weekly. J.E. Atkinson, publisher of the Toronto Star, started this publication in 1910. The Star Weekly ceased publication in 1973.

There is a slight ascent west of 7A Street to reach the corner of 8th Street and 34th Avenue at the southwest corner of the park across from Christ Church Anglican. Near this corner a set of stairs goes up the escarpment slope ending close to the intersection of Pitt Road and Ridge Road. The parish of Christ Church Anglican was formed in 1911 with work on the church building beginning the following year. After two years worshiping in the basement the congregation started construction of the church in 1914. Later additions to the building included the west front and the bell tower followed by the church hall and offices. In 1954, the Archbishop of Canterbury laid the cornerstone for the bell tower. The eight bells in the tower were first rung together in 1957. On the south lawn of the church is a memorial garden where the cremated remains of parishioners can be laid to rest.

From the front of the church, head south along 8th Street with the treed escarpment slope on the right. At 38th Avenue turn left and walk east

Christ Church Anglican in Elbow Park

towards the front entrance of Elbow Park School (3.1 km). As the population of Elbow Park increased, the South Calgary Cottage School was moved to 36th Avenue and 7th Street in 1917 and renamed Elbow Park Cottage School. The cottage school was used until the 1960s with students from Rideau Park School taking general shop and home economics classes in the building. As the community population continued to increase Elbow Park School was constructed in 1926. The building is one of four larger brick schools built between 1926 and 1930. The others are Crescent Heights (1929), Western Canada (1929) and Rideau Park (1930). In WW II the school building was designated as an emergency hospital for the city.

The next section of the walk wanders through the community past an interesting variety of old and new homes. From the northeast corner of the school field turn left and head north on 7th Street to 34th Avenue. Turn right and walk east one block to 6th Street. Turn right and follow 6th Street south back to 38th Avenue. Turn left and follow 38th Avenue east to the traffic lights at Elbow Drive (4.1 km). Cross to the east side of Elbow Drive and continue eastbound to the next corner (5th Street). Turn right and walk south on 5th Street to 40th Avenue. Please note on this side of Elbow Drive some of the streets do not have sidewalks so use caution. The traffic is usually light as there are no through roads.

Turn left and walk east along 40th Avenue. The houses on the south side of 40th Avenue back onto the Elbow River. Near 4A Street there is a very pleasant park along the north bank of the river. Visitors to Stanley Park may recognize the park as the green space you can see across the river from the pathway and picnic area in the park. The author arbitrarily named this park Edison Crescent Park. As you continue east along the north side of the park it narrows near the corner of 40th Avenue and 4th Street. Follow the edge of the park a few steps north from 40th Avenue on 4th Street and then turn right onto Edison Crescent. The park continues east to where Edison Crescent turns left and heads north. There are a few benches and tables in the park. Access to the river in the park is rather limited by the dense growth of trees and bushes along the riverbank.

Your route continues north on Edison Crescent turning left and going west to 4th Street where Edison Crescent ends. Continue straight ahead on 38th Avenue one more block to 4A Street and turn right. At the next corner turn left and follow 37th Avenue west one block to 5th Street. Turn right and walk north one block on 5th Street and turn left onto Elbow Park Lane. A few steps further west will take you back to Elbow Drive (5.7 km). Turn right and head north along the east side of Elbow Drive. At 34th Avenue you reach the south end of J. H. Woods Park. When the path in the park splits take the right branch that leads back to the pedestrian bridge near 32nd Avenue.

Cross the bridge and turn right following Rideau Road back to where the road ends just south of 33rd Avenue. Continue south along the Elbow River Pathway going past the path you came down earlier from Lindsay's Folly. In the next section of path there is a short gradual ascent followed by a gradual descent before you reach the northeast corner of Stanley Park (7.2 km). Across the river are the houses you passed earlier on Edison Crescent.

From the northeast corner of Stanley Park, look for a trail angling up the treed escarpment slope. You will also use this trail on 39th Avenue Walk 2 – Stanley Park, River Park & Sandy Beach. The trail reaches the top of the Heritage Escarpment on 1A Street SW between 38th and 39th Avenue. From here the route begins a short exploration of Parkhill before heading back to the station. Walk north on 1A Street and turn left onto 37th Avenue and then right on 2nd Street. Follow 2nd Street north to 34th Avenue and turn right. At the next corner turn right again and follow 1A Street south to 38th Avenue.

Walk east on 38th Avenue and turn right on Parkhill Street. Follow Parkhill Street south up a short ascent to 38A Avenue and turn left. At the next corner turn right onto Stanley Road and then left onto 39th Avenue. Walk east on 39th Avenue crossing Macleod Trail at the traffic lights and continue a few steps further east to the station (8.9 km).

Route Summary:

1. Walk to the north end of the platform by 39th Avenue.
2. Turn left and walk west one block to Macleod Trail.
3. Cross Macleod Trail at the traffic lights and continue west on 39th Avenue up a slight ascent to Stanley Road.
4. Turn right on Stanley Road and left on 38A Avenue.
5. Walk one long block west on 38A Avenue to 1A Street SW and the top of the Heritage Escarpment.
6. Follow a trail to the right along the top of the escarpment to Princess Obolensky Park just east of 4th Street.
7. Walk north on 4th Street and turn left on a path crossing a green space on the north side of the Southern Alberta Pioneers building.
8. Follow the path down the escarpment taking the left branch at a junction.
9. At the bottom of the escarpment turn right on the Elbow River Pathway.
10. When the path ends continue north on Rideau Road to 32nd Avenue.
11. Turn right on 32nd Avenue and then left along an unnamed road/alley in front of Rideau Park School.
12. From the front of the school follow 31st Avenue back to Rideau Road and turn left walking a short distance to the pedestrian bridge on your right.
13. Cross the bridge and continue straight ahead using the pedestrian light to cross to the west side of Elbow Drive.
14. Continue straight ahead on 32nd Avenue.
15. Turn left at 7th Street and walk south to 34th Avenue.
16. Turn right and walk west on 34th Avenue to 8th Street.
17. Turn left and walk south on 8th Street to 38th Avenue.
18. Turn left and walk east one block on 38th Avenue.
19. Turn left on 7th Street and walk north to 34th Avenue.
20. Turn right and walk east on 34th Avenue to 6th Street.
21. Turn right and walk south on 6th Street to 38th Avenue.
22. Turn left following 38th Avenue east across Elbow Drive at the traffic lights and continue eastbound to 5th Street.
23. Turn right walking south on 5th Street to 40th Avenue.
24. Walk east on 40th Avenue to 4th Street.
25. Take a few steps to the left on 4th Street and turn right on Edison Crescent.
26. Follow Edison Crescent east, north and west to where it ends at 4th Street and 38th Avenue.
27. Continue straight ahead on 38th Avenue to 4A Street and turn right.
28. Walk one block north and turn left on 37th Avenue.
29. Walk one block west and turn right on 5th Street.
30. Walk north on 5th Street and turn left on Elbow Park Lane and walk a few steps west to Elbow Drive.

31. Turn right and follow Elbow Drive north to the south end of J.H. Woods Park at 34th Avenue.
32. Follow the park path taking the right branch at a junction to return to the pedestrian bridge.
33. Cross the bridge and retrace your steps back to the beginning of the path at the south end of Rideau Road.
34. Follow the path until you reach the northeast corner of Stanley Park.
35. Follow a trail on your left up the escarpment slope to 1A Street between 38th and 39th Avenues.
36. Walk north on 1A Street and turn left on 37th Avenue.
37. At the next corner turn right on 2nd Street.
38. Follow 2nd Street north and turn right on 34th Avenue.
39. At the next corner turn right and follow 1A Street back to 38th Avenue.
40. Turn left and follow 38th Avenue to Parkhill Street.
41. Turn left and follow Parkhill Street south to 38A Avenue.
42. Turn left and follow 38A Avenue east to Stanley Road.
43. Turn right and follow Stanley Road to 39th Avenue.
44. Turn left and retrace your earlier route back across Macleod Trail to the station.

39th Avenue Walk 2
Stanley Park, River Park & Sandy Beach

Walk Overview: This mostly out-and-back route goes down the Heritage Escarpment on the west side of the Parkhill community and then travels in a southwesterly direction passing through Stanley Park, River Park and Sandy Beach. The turn around point is at the north end of Glenmore Dam. Points of interest include the three parks, the mix of older and new homes and the views from the different escarpments.

Length: 10.1 km

Route Description & Accessibility: The accessibility for this route is very poor. You descend the Heritage Escarpment on a trail and near the end of the route ascend the same trail. You also ascend a rough and steep trail from Sandy Beach to River Park and on the return section you descend a steep path. The third long up and down section is the Britannia Escarpment with an ascent on a rough trail and a descent on a path. No alternate routes for these ascents/descents are included in the text.

Food and Drink: Stanley Park and Sandy Beach have picnic tables.

74

Washrooms: Stanley Park and Sandy Beach have seasonal public washrooms.

Map References: Clear-View – 36 & 42, MapArt – 164 & 174
Rand McNally – 59 & 66, Sherlock – 35 & 34

Route Category: Walk – The route starts and ends at the station (no bus is required).

The Walk: From the north end of the platform turn left on 39th Avenue and walk west one block to Macleod Trail. Cross Macleod Trail at the traffic lights and continue west on 39th Avenue up a slight ascent to Stanley Road on the east side of the Parkhill/Stanley Park Community Association Park. Turn right on Stanley Road and left on 38A Avenue. Walk one long block west on 38A Avenue to 1A Street SW. Cross to the west side of 1A Street and turn left on the top of the Heritage Escarpment overlooking the Elbow River and the east side of Elbow Park across the river. Follow a dirt trail south beside the road for a short distance and turn right on a trail leading down the slope to the Elbow River Pathway.

The trail joins the pathway at the northeast corner of Stanley Park. This 21 hectares park was designated as park space in the 1920s. The picnic area adjacent to the river was developed in the 1950s (0.9 km). The origin of the park name is unknown. The facilities in the park include picnic tables with BBQ stands, playground areas, sports fields, tennis courts, seasonal washrooms, an outdoor swimming pool with wading pool, lawn bowling and flower gardens.

The route continues west along the Elbow River Pathway leaving the park at the northwest corner. Across the river is Edison Crescent Park that was on the previous walk. After leaving the park the pathway is on the north side of Riverdale Avenue. When the path reaches Elbow Drive and Elboya Bridge follow the path under the bridge (1.4 km). If the river level is high this underpass may be closed.

On the west side of the bridge the path continues through a green space before turning left and going up a slight ascent to Riverdale Avenue. Turn right and continue west on Riverdale Avenue. Several sidewalk stamps on the south side of Riverdale are dated 1930. At 8th Street the Sifton Boulevard pedestrian bridge is on your right. Riverdale Avenue changes direction slightly to the left at this point. Continue to follow Riverdale Avenue until it reaches a parking lot at the north end of Riverdale Park (2.5 km).

A paved path heads south from the parking lot through a natural area with a mixture of grassland, trees and shrubs. You have the option to follow a trail that starts by the parking lot and wanders through the riverine forest

Flower Gardens at Stanley Park

beside the Elbow River. This trail can be a bit overgrown or muddy at times and sometimes splits into more than one branch. The trail is also a bit isolated so use your own discretion about walking alone. The trail joins the paved path by the Sandy Beach pedestrian bridge (2.9 km). On the left as you follow the path from the parking lot is the Britannia Escarpment with several trails leading to the top of the slope on the west side of Britannia Drive. On the return portion of this walk the route will climb the escarpment.

After crossing the pedestrian bridge the route enters Sandy Beach Park. This 21 hectares area was preserved for park use in the 1940s with development taking place in the 1950s. The footbridge was added at that time. The facilities in the park include picnic areas and a shelter, firepits and BBQ stands, playground areas and seasonal washrooms.

A short distance from the bridge a trail branches off to the right and climbs up the escarpment to River Park. When coaching young track club runners many years ago I was told this trail was called *Cow Path*. Follow the trail to the top of the slope to a trail extending in a north-south direction along the top of the escarpment in River Park (3.1 km). In 1953 Colonel Eric Harvie donated 24 hectares on top of the escarpment for use as a park. Harvie was a Calgary lawyer, businessman and philanthropist who founded the Devonian Group of Charitable Foundations. This group was a major participant in the development of Calgary's river pathway system. A pedestrian bridge on the Bow River just downstream of Carburn Park in Riverbend is named for Eric Harvie. He also played a major role in the development of Heritage Park. Development of River Park started in 1956 and was mostly completed by 1960. The park was first named Riverview Park.

The park is one of the more popular off-leash parks in south Calgary. A short distance north of where you reached the top of the escarpment is a small memorial park named the Catherine (Cat) Margetts Memorial Park. She died in a fire in 2004 while attempting to rescue animals from her burning home. In a park widely used by dog owners, this memorial area is a fitting tribute to this young woman who operated a dog walking business.

From the top of the escarpment turn left and follow the trail south to 50th Avenue where there is a parking area for park users. Cross to the south side of 50th Avenue and turn right (3.7 km). Follow a paved path a few steps west and turn left following the path south past the west side of Emily Folinsbee School. Emily Folinsbee was elected as the first secretary of the Calgary Association for Retarded Children (now the Calgary Association for the Mentally Handicapped). Christine Meikle founded the association in 1952. Emily Folinsbee volunteered at the home school opened in 1953 by Christine Meikle. Christine Meikle School opened in Bridgeland/Riverside in 1958. Four years later Emily Folinsbee School opened on this site. In 1969 the Calgary Board of Education absorbed both schools.

The route continues south from the school following the path along the top of the escarpment. Across the river is the Calgary Golf and Country Club. When the path splits with the right branch leading away from the top of the escarpment follow the left branch. Near this junction is Safety City, operated by the Calgary Safety Council. This facility allows young children to experience driving mini-cars through a network of streets with traffic lights and stop signs.

Shortly after the junction the route passes a fenced off area containing the buildings of the Glenmore Water Treatment Plant. The path then goes down a short descent to the north end of Glenmore Dam (4.6 km). A path can be followed across the top of the dam and over a bridge to the south side of Glenmore Trail. Heritage Walk 1 - East Glenmore Park & Heritage Town Square turns around on the other side of Glenmore Trail.

Glenmore is a Gaelic word meaning "Big Valley". Sam Livingston was an early settler in this area with his homestead of the same name being located upstream from the dam. Most of the land he owned was submerged under the waters of the reservoir when Glenmore Dam was constructed in the 1930s. The Livingston home is now one of the buildings in Heritage Park.

Elbow River Pathway in Sandy Beach Park

From the north end of the dam follow a second path up a small ascent on the right on the north side of the reservoir. At the top of this small ascent is a rest area with several benches and a series of information plaques about the water treatment plant.

Turn around at this point and retrace the route back to the path on the north side of Emily Folinsbee School beside 50th Avenue. Turn right and follow this path east crossing the access road down into Sandy Beach Park. Stay to the right on this path down the slope as cyclists share the path with pedestrians. The path splits at the bottom of the slope beside a parking lot with the cyclists taking the left branch. Follow the right branch past a larger parking lot and turn left when the path turns west beside the river (6.3 km). Across the river is the very steep Britannia Escarpment.

The path stays beside the river as it passes the picnic areas for the park. The washroom building is up a short set of stairs beside the park shelter. A short distance before the bridge the bicycle path joins your path from the left. In a few steps more you reach the junction where *Cow Path* heads up the slope.

Cross the bridge (6.6 km) and angle to the right in a southeasterly direction. Follow a trail on the long climb to the top of the escarpment. The trail reaches the top of the escarpment near Britannia Drive and 49th Avenue (7.1 km) in Britannia. The shops of Britannia Shopping Centre are just one block east of this location. Of trivial interest is the connection the names of some of the streets in Britannia have with royalty. The names include Britannia, Coronation, Crown, Elizabeth, Charles, Anne and Imperial.

Turn left and walk along the grass on the top of the escarpment beside Britannia Drive. The route will come to houses on the left backing onto the escarpment slope. Continue along the sidewalk in front of the houses. A few houses past Elizabeth Road there is a path on the left leading down the slope between houses. It may be a little difficult to find this path as you walk along the edge of a private driveway to reach the path. At the bottom of the slope the path ends on Lansdowne Avenue at 10th Street. Turn right and follow Lansdowne Avenue east to 8th Street. Make a slight jog to the right and turn left to continue east on Lansdowne Avenue. At this point the treed escarpment is on the right. This section of Lansdowne Avenue has the feel of walking down a country lane. On one walk along this street I spotted a deer at the base of the slope.

Just before Elbow Drive turn left and follow the sidewalk along the edge of the traffic circle to Riverdale Avenue. Cross to the north side of Riverdale Avenue onto the Elbow River Pathway (8.6 km). From here retrace the earlier route back to the station (10.1 km).

Route Summary:

1. Walk to the north end of the platform at 39th Avenue.
2. Turn left and walk west one block to Macleod Trail.
3. Cross Macleod Trail at the traffic lights and continue west on 39th Avenue to Stanley Road.
4. Turn right at Stanley Road and then left at 38A Avenue.
5. Walk one long block west to the top of the escarpment on 1A Street.
6. Cross to the west side of 1A Street and turn left following a trail along the top of the escarpment.
7. Follow a trail leading down the escarpment to join the Elbow River Pathway at the northeast corner of Stanley Park.
8. Follow the path along the north side of the park to the northwest corner at Riverdale Avenue and 4th Street.
9. Continue on the path along the north side of Riverdale Avenue to Elbow Drive.
10. Follow the path under Elboya Bridge to the west side of Elbow Drive.
11. On the west side of the bridge the path continues through a green space and turns left up a slight ascent to Riverdale Avenue.
12. Turn right and follow Riverdale Avenue west to a parking lot at the end of the road.
13. The path continues from the parking lot to the Sandy Beach pedestrian bridge.

14. Cross the bridge and turn left on the path.
15. Turn right onto a trail leading up the escarpment to River Park.
16. Turn left and follow a trail south through River Park to 50th Avenue.
17. Cross to the south side of 50th Avenue and turn right on the path.
18. Walk a few steps west and turn left on a path leading south past the west side of Emily Folinsbee School.
19. At a junction take the left branch along the top of the escarpment.
20. The path goes down a slight descent to the north end of Glenmore Dam.
21. From the north end of the dam turn right and follow another path a few steps up a slight ascent and turn right to a rest area with benches and a series of information plaques.
22. From here retrace the route back to the path on 50th Avenue on the north side of the school.
23. Turn right and follow the path east crossing over an access road for Sandy Beach.
24. Follow the path down the escarpment slope to Sandy Beach.
25. At a junction at the bottom of the slope take the right branch leading past a large parking lot and turning left by the river.
26. Follow the path beside the river back to the pedestrian bridge.
27. After crossing the bridge angle to the right and follow a trail that ascends the escarpment slope.
28. The trail ends at the top of the slope just west of Britannia Drive near 49th Avenue.
29. Walk north along the top of the escarpment until you reach the first house backing onto the slope.
30. Continue along Britannia Drive in front of the houses.
31. A few houses past Elizabeth Road there is a path on the left leading down the slope between houses to Lansdowne Avenue. It may be a little difficult to find this path as you walk along the edge of a private driveway to reach the path.
32. Turn right and follow Lansdowne Avenue east to 8th Street.
33. Make a slight jog to the right and continue on Lansdowne Avenue.
34. Just before Elbow Drive turn left and follow the sidewalk along the edge of the traffic circle to Riverdale Avenue.
35. Cross to the north side of Riverdale Avenue and rejoin the Elbow River Pathway in the green space on the west side of Elbow Drive.
36. From here retrace the route back to the station.

Chapter Four
Chinook Station

Station Information: The station is located in the light industrial area of Manchester Industrial South on the south side of 61st Avenue between 1A Street SW and Centre Street. At the time of writing the station is closed until the fall of 2013 for construction of a new station with a platform for four car trains. During construction a shuttle bus will operate from 39th Avenue to connect with the bus routes that stop at Chinook Station. The shuttle bus frequency will be 10 minutes daily at mid-day.

All four of the walks in this chapter include a bus ride to the start of the route and a bus ride from the end of the route back to the station. The station is in a location that is not suitable for good walking routes.

Chinook Walk 1
North Glenmore Park

Walk Overview: This route starts at the west end of North Glenmore Park near 37th Street and 66th Avenue SW. After an out-and-back descent and ascent of the escarpment slope in Weaselhead Flats Natural Area the linear portion of the route follows a paved path along the top of the escarpment in North Glenmore Park. The route finishes with a short section through North Glenmore Park community east of Crowchild Trail. The section of the route in Weaselhead Flats is isolated so use your own discretion about walking alone.

Length: 6.1 km

Route Description & Accessibility: The escarpment slope descent/ascent between North Glenmore Park and Weaselhead Flats Natural Area has poor accessibility. There is no alternate route in the text for this escarpment slope. The section of the route in North Glenmore Park is relatively flat. As you near the bus stop at the end of the route there is a short section on grass that may limit accessibility.

Food and Drink: North Glenmore Park has several picnic areas as well as benches at the top of the escarpment overlooking the Glenmore Reservoir. Near the end of the route there is a bakery and places to buy food in Lakeview Plaza on the west side of Crowchild Trail just north of 66th Avenue.

Washrooms: There are pit toilet buildings and a seasonal washroom building in North Glenmore Park.

Map References: Clear-View – 41 & 42, MapArt – 173 & 174 Rand McNally – 65 & 66, Sherlock – 39 & 40

Route Category: Bus/Walk/Bus – Ride the bus to the start of the route and when finished the walk ride the bus back to the station.

Bus Directions from the station to the start of the walk: Catch bus # 47 Lakeview at stop 5990 by the station. During the construction of the station this bus will use the temporary stop 4447 on 3rd Street between 60th and 61st Avenues. Get off at stop 4597 on westbound 66th Avenue at Lethbridge Crescent. This stop is 16 minutes from the station. The bus frequency is 45 minutes daily during mid-day.

The Walk: From the bus stop continue west on 66th Avenue to the intersection with 37th Street. On the left is the access road leading into North Glenmore Park. Cross 37th Street and walk straight ahead across the parking lot for North Glenmore Park and Weaselhead Flats Natural Area. On the west side of the parking lot is a pit toilet building. Continue straight ahead on a paved path crossing over the bike path and then turning right on the walking path. There are two paved paths on the top of the escarpment throughout North Glenmore Park with the walking path being closer to the edge of the escarpment slope.

In a short distance you reach a viewpoint area with information plaques (0.4 km). From the viewpoint there is a panoramic view of the Glenmore Reservoir. The land around the reservoir was set aside for park use in the mid 1950s with the access road through the park being constructed in the early 1960s about the same time as Lakeview community north of the park was being developed. The name Glenmore comes from a Gaelic word meaning *Big Valley*.

From the viewpoint a single path continues west a few steps before descending the escarpment slope into the Weaselhead Flats Natural Area. Keep to the right and watch for cyclists. Follow the path as it heads south from the bottom of the escarpment to a pedestrian bridge across the Elbow River (0.9 km). The path and trails on the other side of the river are included in Heritage Station Walk 3 – Weaselhead Flats Natural Area.

From the bridge retrace your steps back up the escarpment slope and along the top of the escarpment taking the right hand path at the junction east of the viewpoint. Follow the path east through North Glenmore Park past several picnic areas and parking lots. There is a washroom building

West end of Glenmore Reservoir

in the picnic area closest to the 37th Street end of the park and a pit toilet building partway through the park beside the path (2.9 km). There is an excellent view of Glenmore Reservoir as you walk along the path. On the far side of the reservoir are South Glenmore Park and the communities of Oakridge and Bayview.

When the path reaches the end of the south-facing escarpment (3.8 km), make a left turn and head north past the blue roofed clubhouse of Glenmore Canoe and Rowing Club. After passing the clubhouse you can see a new wetlands area on the west side of the park access road near the northeast corner of North Glenmore Park. The separate walking and cycling path become a single path just before exiting the park. Continue north on the east side of Crowchild Trail with Lakeview Village on the left and Earl Grey Golf Club on the right.

At 66th Avenue the path angles to the right away from Crowchild Trail and heads in a northeasterly direction through the small community of North Glenmore Park (5.0 km). The area for this community was annexed in 1956 with residential development beginning the next year. In the early 1900s

Glenmore Canoe & Rowing Clubhouse

there was a sandstone quarry in the area that is now the community.

Cross Longridge Drive and continue on the path until you reach the same road again near the North Glenmore Park Community Association Hall. Turn left and follow Longridge Drive west. The community park and the Calgary Girls School are on the right. Longridge Drive ends when it meets Larkspur Way. Turn right and walk north past the school to where Larkspur Way ends and Lombardy Crescent starts on your left. Continue straight ahead towards a traffic wall on the south side of Glenmore Trail and turn left behind the houses on the north side of Lombardy Crescent. Walk west through the grass area to where you angle to the right to reach the bus stop.

Bus Directions from the end of the route to the station:

Catch bus # 47 Chinook at stop 6206 on northbound Crowchild Trail just south of Glenmore Trail (6.1 km). Get off the bus at stop 5990 back at the station. During the construction of the station this bus will use temporary stop 4447 on 3rd Street between 60th and 61st Avenues. The scheduled time back to the station is 12 minutes. The bus frequency is 45 minutes daily at mid-day.

Route Summary:

1. Catch bus # 47 Lakeview/Chinook and get off at the stop on westbound 66th Avenue near Lethbridge Crescent.

2. Walk west on 66th Avenue to 37th Street and cross to the west side.
3. Walk straight ahead through a parking lot.
4. Continue straight ahead on a path crossing the bike path and turn right on the walking path.
5. In a few steps you reach a viewpoint area with information plaques.
6. From the viewpoint a single path leads down the slope.
7. The path leads to a pedestrian bridge across the Elbow River.
8. Retrace the route back up the slope to where you first joined the walking path.
9. Follow the path east along the top of the escarpment.
10. When the path reaches the end of the south facing escarpment slope make a left turn and head north.
11. As you pass the Earl Grey Golf Club on the right the cycling and walking paths join.
12. Walk north along the east side of Crowchild Trail.
13. At 66th Avenue turn right on a path angling away from Crowchild Trail.
14. Cross Longridge Drive twice before reaching North Glenmore Park Community Hall.
15. Turn left and walk west along Longridge Road and turn right on Larkspur Way on the west side of the Calgary Girls School.
16. Continue straight ahead towards a traffic wall on the south side of Glenmore Trail.
17. Turn left and walk west through a green space with the wall on the right and the back of the houses on Lombardy Crescent on the left.
18. Continue west through the green space to where you catch bus # 47 on the east side of Crowchild Trail.

Chinook Walk 2
Carburn Park & Riverbend

Walk Overview: This route begins with a combination of out-and-back and loop sections in Carburn Park on the west side of the community of Riverbend. This 135 hectares park comprising largely riverine forest beside the Bow River opened in 1986 on a former Burnco gravel pit site. Carburn Aggregates, owned by J.F. Burns and Clayton Carroll, was the original owner of the land. This company merged with several companies in 1969 to form Burnco Industries Limited. The three ponds in the park were developed in former gravel extraction pits. After leaving the park the route has an out-and-back section beside the Bow River on the west side of Riverbend and concludes with a linear section through Riverbend to the end of the walk.

Length: 6.4 km

Route Description & Accessibility: Accessibility is very good on this relatively flat route. The walking surface is on paved paths with a few short sections on sidewalk.

Food and Drink: There is a picnic area beside the largest pond in Carburn Park. Riverbend Centre adjacent to the bus stop at the end of the walk has a grocery store and restaurants.

Washrooms: There is a seasonal washroom adjacent to Carburn Park parking lot. In the picnic area of the park there is a pit toilet building.

Map References: Clear-View – 50 & 44, MapArt – 174
Rand McNally – 76 & 68, Sherlock – 42

Route Category: Bus/Walk/Bus – Ride the bus to the start of the route and when finished the walk ride the bus back to the station.

Bus Directions from the station to the start of the walk:
Catch bus # 36 Riverbend at stop 6451 at the station. During the construction of the station this bus will use the temporary stop 4439 on 3rd Street between 59th and 60th Avenues. Get off at stop 8056 on eastbound Riverbend Drive at Riverview Drive. This stop is 12 minutes from the station daily. The bus frequency is 45 minutes daily at mid-day.

The Walk: After getting off the bus walk back a few steps on Riverbend Drive and turn left onto Riverview Drive. Riverview Drive leads south to the access road into Carburn Park across from Dream View Village (0.3 km).

Follow the paved path past the parking lot to the south pond, the smallest of the three ponds in the park. There is a service building beside the pond with a seasonal washroom. A map of the park is located beside the parking lot. Continue on the paved path past the small pond to a junction at the southeast corner of the middle pond (0.7 km). The paved path extending the length of the park is part of the Bow River Pathway. Use caution if there are cyclists in the area. Take the right branch at this junction and continue north along the east side of the middle pond. A treed area on the right separates you from the houses on the west side of Riverbend. At the junction at the north end of the pond again take the right branch (1.2 km). The path leads to the north pond in the park.

Continue on the path along the east side of the north pond to where the path goes under Graves Bridge on Glenmore Trail. This is the turn around point (2.0 km). Chinook Walk 3 – Lynnwood Ridge and Beaverdam Flats Park passes by the north side of the bridge. Graves Bridge is named for Arthur G. Graves who immigrated to Canada from England in 1897 and served as a city alderman from 1905 to 1908, Graves was a city commissioner from 1908 to 1921 and again from 1923 to 1932. The bridge opened in 1970 with Graves being present for the official opening. A second bridge has now been added to handle the heavy volume of traffic on Glenmore Trail.

Prior to the heavy flooding along the river in 2005 there was a narrow trail along the west side of the north pond between the pond and the river. However portions of this trail were washed out in the flooding. Retrace the route back to the junction at the north end of the middle pond. Take the right junction and head south along the west side of the pond. This path goes past the picnic area (3.3 km) and the portable washroom building. There is an extensive network of trails between this path and the riverbank. These trails are isolated so use your own discretion about walking alone in this area of the park. On visits to the park, I have spotted deer and a coyote along these trails. Along the riverbank you may be fortunate enough to spot a bald eagle. Watch for pelicans in the summer months.

At the junction at the south end of the middle pond retrace your steps past the south pond to the parking lot. Follow the paved path past the

Middle pond at Carburn Park

parking lot and turn right on Riverview Drive. When the road ends continue south on the path to a small gazebo beside the east end of the Eric Harvie pedestrian bridge (4.3 km). Eric Harvie's success in the oil industry enabled him to start the Glenbow Foundation in 1955. In 1966 his vast collection of artifacts was donated to the Alberta Government, marking the beginning of the Glenbow Alberta Institute. Sue Higgins Park (formerly Southland Park), a popular dog walking area, is on the west side of the bridge. Canyon Meadows Walk 3 – Mallard Point to Eric Harvie Bridge turns around on the other side of the bridge in Sue Higgins Park.

The route continues south from the gazebo in Riverbend Park. Continue south past two junctions to a row of large rocks extending east at right angles to the path (4.9 km) at the southwest corner of the community of Riverbend. The row of rocks is the turn around point. The former gravel pit south of this point is being developed as the community of Quarry Park with a mix of housing and office buildings. When the pathway south of the large rocks is completed this route can be extended into the riverbank area on the west side of Quarry Park. Retrace the route to the junction closer to Eric Harvie Bridge where a right turn leads in a northeasterly direction through a

Gazebo by Eric Harvie Bridge

green space between houses (5.2 km).

This path leads into to an area with playing fields, Riverbend School and Riverbend Community Hall. Follow the path to the corner of 18th Street and Rivervalley Drive. Turn left and walk north on 18th Street to Riverbend Gate and cross to the northeast corner of the intersection. Riverglen Drive extends east on this side of 18th Street. North of Riverglen Drive is Riverbend Centre with a variety of refreshment choices (a large chain grocery store and several restaurants).

Bus Directions from the end of the route back to the station: Catch bus # 41 Lynnwood at stop 8064 on northbound 18th Street at Riverglen Drive. Get off at stop 6451 back at the station. During the construction of the station this bus will use the temporary stop 4439 on 3rd Street between 59th and 60th Avenues. The scheduled time back to the station is 11 minutes on weekdays and Saturdays. The bus frequency is 45 minutes at mid-day on weekdays and Saturdays. Please note that bus # 41 does not operate on Sundays. On Sundays catch bus # 36 Riverbend at stop 8064 on northbound 18th Street at Riverglen Drive. This bus will then travel through Lynnwood before returning to the station.

Route Summary:

1. Catch bus # 36 Riverbend and get off at the stop on eastbound Riverbend Drive just past Riverview Drive.
2. After getting off the bus walk back a few steps on Riverbend Drive and turn left onto Riverview Drive.
3. Follow the road south to the access road into Carburn Park.
4. Follow the path to the right past the parking lot and the south pond.
5. Continue on the path to a junction at the southeast corner of the middle pond.
6. Take the right branch and head north along the east side of the middle pond.
7. At the junction at the north end of the middle pond take the right branch leading to the north pond.
8. The turn around point is just south of where the path goes under Graves Bridge on Glenmore Trail.
9. Retrace the route back to the junction at the north end of the middle pond.
10. Take the right branch heading south on the west side of the pond.
11. At the junction at the southeast corner of the middle pond retrace the route past the south pond and parking lot to Riverview Drive.
12. Turn right and walk south along Riverview Drive and continue on the path when the road ends.
13. The path leads to a junction on the east side of Eric Harvie Bridge.

14. Continue south from the bridge until the path ends by some large rocks at the southwest corner of Riverview.
15. Retrace the route back to the path junction closest to the bridge and turn right.
16. The path heads northeasterly through a green space and ends near the corner of 18th Street and Rivervalley Drive.
17. Turn left and walk north on 18th Street to Riverbend Gate on the left and Riverglen Drive on the right.
18. Cross to the northeast corner of the intersection and catch bus # 41 Lynnwood a few steps north of Riverglen Drive.

Chinook Walk 3
Lynnwood Ridge & Beaverdam Flats Park

Walk Overview: This loop route starts at the south end of Lynnwood Ridge and follows the path along the top of the escarpment on the west side of the community. After you descend the escarpment slope into Beaverdam Flats Park, the return portion of the walk follows a trail beside the Bow River and ends in Ogden. The section of the route in Beaverdam Flats Park and along the riverbank is isolated so use your own discretion about walking alone.

Length: 5.9 km

Route Description & Accessibility: Accessibility is very poor in the second half of this route. Only the paved path along the top of the escarpment on the west side of Lynnwood Ridge offers good accessibility. The walking surface for the route is a mix of paved paths, sidewalks, trails and grass. No alternate route for the escarpment slope or the uneven trail by the river is included in the text.

Food and Drink: Beaverdam Flats Park has picnic tables set amidst the trees throughout the park. Glenmore Square shopping centre near the end of the route has a grocery store and restaurants.

Washrooms: There are no public washrooms along this route.

Map References: Clear-View – 44, MapArt – 174
Rand McNally – 69, Sherlock – 42 & 36

Route Category: Bus/Walk/Bus – Ride the bus to the start of the route and when finished the walk ride the bus back to the station.

Bus Directions from the station to the start of the walk:
Catch bus # 41 Lynnwood at stop 6451 at the station. During the construction at the station use the temporary bus stop 4439 on 3rd Street

between 59th and 60th Avenues. Get off at stop 8199 on northbound 18th Street just north of Lytton Crescent. This stop is 8 minutes from the station. The bus frequency is 45 minutes daily at mid-day except on Sunday. The Lynnwood bus does not operate on Sundays. You will need to catch bus # 36 Riverbend that services Riverbend prior to entering Lynnwood.

The Walk: After getting off the bus walk south on 18th Street and turn right onto Lysander Drive. At the point where Lysander Drive turns north there is a paved path to follow to reach the main path along the top of the escarpment (0.4 km). This main path is part of the Bow River Pathway. Turn right and walk north on the path.

From the path there are excellent views of downtown and of the Bow River at the base of the escarpment. After you pass some apartment buildings there is a viewpoint with an information plaque overlooking Beaverdam Flats Park at the base of the escarpment. The main parking lot for the park is just north of the viewpoint (1.5 km).

In 1890 Canadian Pacific Railway purchased a portion of the land now occupied by the park. Patrick Burns bought the land ten years later and sold it in 1929. Imperial Oil then purchased the west portion in 1957 and subsequently purchased the east portion the following year. The city then purchased a 14.6 hectares parcel of land in 1973 for use as parkland.

A few steps north of the viewpoint follow the path down a steep descent

Pond in Beaverdam Flats Park

into the park. Keep to the right as cyclists also use this path. There is a pond area at the bottom of the path where there may be waterfowl.

The paved path makes a left turn by the pond area. There is a junction just past the pond. Make a right turn at the junction and follow the path north through the park. At the next junction turn right on the path. The area to the right extending to the base of the escarpment had to undergo extensive reclamation some years ago to remove contaminated soil caused by leakage from the refinery tanks that used to be located at the top of the escarpment on the north side of Lynnwood Ridge. On Chinook Walk 4 – Ogden & Millican Estates the route passes a former residential area at the top of the escarpment where houses and apartments had to be removed because of contaminated soil.

Near the north end of the park there is a small shelter building. The turn around point of the walk is just north of the shelter at the Canadian National Railway Bridge at the north end of the park (2.5 km). Beyond the bridge some of the area is still fenced off because of the leakage from more refinery tanks. Ironically that area is called Old Refinery Park. Retrace the route from the bridge back to a junction with a trail leading to the right (3.0

Sappers Bridge in Beaverdam Flats Park

km). Follow this trail as it heads south on the west side of the park. Ignore any trails leading to the left or right. There are picnic tables scattered through the trees along this trail.

At the south end of the park take the right branch at a junction. This trail leads to the small wooden Sappers Bridge (4.0 km). The original Sappers Bridge in this location was constructed by a group of soldiers from the 33rd Engineers Squadron. A *sapper* is a name used for military field engineers. The original bridge was damaged during the extensive flooding along the river in 2005.

Cross the bridge and climb a few stairs. Turn right and follow a somewhat rough trail south between the base of the escarpment and the river. Most of this trail is in an open area. City crews placed many large rocks along the riverbank some years ago to try and prevent further erosion. The trail then enters a treed area that can be overgrown at times. The trail leads to a paved path on the north side of Graves Bridge (5.0 km). The right branch leads under the bridge to the turnaround point for Chinook Walk 2 – Carburn Park & Riverbend.

Your route follows the left branch of the path up a short ascent to the edge of Ogden Drive. Turn right and follow the grass along the edge of Ogden Drive back to 18th Street. Near the last house on Ogden Drive angle to the right across the grass to the sidewalk on 18th Street just south of 76th Avenue. The bus stop is just south of 76th Avenue.

Bus Directions from the end of the route to the station:
Catch bus # 41 Riverbend at stop 6132 on the southwest corner of 18th Street and 76th Avenue (5.9 km). The scheduled time back to the station is 8 minutes. The bus frequency is 45 minutes daily at mid-day. Get off at stop 6451 back at the station. During the construction of the station the bus will use temporary stop 4439 on 3rd Street between 59th and 60th Avenues.

Route Summary:
1. Catch bus # 41 Lynnwood and get off at the stop on northbound 18th Street just north of Lytton Crescent. On Sundays catch bus # 36 Riverbend.
2. Walk south on 18th Street and turn right on Lysander Drive.
3. Follow Lysander Drive west and when it turns right to head north follow a path leading across the grass to the top of the escarpment slope.
4. Turn right and follow the path north to a viewpoint with an information plaque near the Beaverdam Flats Park parking lot.
5. Follow the path down the escarpment past a pond area.
6. At a junction make a right turn following the path north through the park.
7. At the next junction go right on the path.
8. The turn around point is the large black railway bridge at the north end of

the park.

9. Retrace the route back to the last junction and turn right on a trail.
10. Follow this trail to the south end of the park. Ignore any trails to the left or right.
11. At the south end of the park follow the right trail at a junction.
12. The trail leads to Sappers Bridge (a small wooden bridge).
13. Cross the bridge and climb a few stairs. Turn right and follow a rough trail south between the base of the escarpment and the river.
14. At the south end of the open area the trail enters a treed area that can be overgrown at times.
15. The trail leads to a junction with the path on the north side of Glenmore Trail.
16. Take the left branch up a short ascent to the edge of Ogden Drive.
17. Turn right and walk along the grass beside Ogden Drive.
18. Near the last house on Ogden Drive angle to the right across the grass to the sidewalk on 18th Street just south of 76th Avenue.
19. Catch bus # 36 Lynnwood on the southwest corner of 18th Street and 76th Avenue.

Chinook Walk 4
Ogden & Millican Estates

Walk Overview: This route is a large loop. Ogden and Millican Estates are two of the oldest communities in Calgary. In 1912-13 Canadian Pacific Railway opened Ogden Shops on the east side of the present-day community some 4.6 miles from the centre of Calgary. Twelve shop buildings were developed on the site including the main locomotive shop, a tender and wheel shop, a pattern shop and storage, a foundry, stores department and offices, oil house, planing mill, power house, freight car heavy repair shop, mess hall and apprentice class room, and mess hall staff quarters and a scrap dock. The total area of the buildings was slightly less than 500,000 square feet or approximately 11.5 acres. The shops and community were named for I.G. Ogden, a former Vice-president of the railway. On May 12th, 1912, the Morning Albertan newspaper ran this ad under the name of The Canadian Pacific Townsite, next to the Canadian Pacific's Giant Railway Industrial Plant. "On Tuesday, May 28th at 9 am, the Department of Natural Resources, Canadian Pacific Railway, will place on the market twenty-eight hundred lots in Ogden adjacent to the Company's new five million dollar car shops now under construction". The ad said "although Ogden lies within the corporate limits of Calgary it will in reality be a city in itself, with its own business district and residence area – a prosperous city with prosperous inhabitants. Each month the CPR will be distributing a payroll totaling thousands of dollars to five thousand employees of the Ogden Shops. This alone is assurance that Ogden will prosper".

The promoters were looking to make a quick profit, but some CPR employees purchased the unwanted land from the railway and resold it at a profit. Other communities were developing at this time and not all the CPR employees were choosing to live in the Ogden area. A street railway line was laid as far as 82nd Avenue on South Hill (the area just south of present-day Glenmore Trail) making it easier for workers to travel to the shops. Lots in Ogden dropped from $300 to $25 and the real estate boom in the community soon ended.

Millican Estates north of Ogden is named for the Millican family who settled in this area in the early 1900s. As you explore the two communities the large amount of green space becomes evident. This route will pass some older churches, a former hotel built prior to WWI and several parks named after former community residents.

Length: 6.3 km

Route Description & Accessibility: Most of this route is relatively flat with good accessibility. There is a gradual ascent between Ogden and Millican Estates. Near the end of the route there is a steep descent on a grass slope that has poor accessibility. No alternate route for this slope is included in the text. The walking surface for the route is mostly sidewalks with some sections on grass.

Food and Drink: There is a grocery store and restaurants at Glenmore Square near the start and end of the route. Partway through the route you pass a corner store.

Washrooms: There are no public washrooms along the route.

Map References: Clear-View – 45, MapArt – 175
Rand McNally – 69, Sherlock – 42 & 36

Route Category: Bus/Walk/Bus – Ride the bus to the start of the route and when finished the walk ride the bus back to the station.

Bus Directions from the station to the start of the walk:

Catch bus # 41 Lynnwood at stop 6451 at the station. During the construction of the station use temporary stop 4439 on 3rd Street between 59th and 60th Avenues. Get off at stop 6137 on northbound 18th Street just north of 76th Avenue. This stop is 7 minutes from the station. The bus frequency is 45 minutes daily at mid-day except on Sundays. On Sundays catch bus # 36 Riverbend that services Riverbend before travelling into Lynnwood as bus # 41 Lynnwood does not operate that day.

The Walk: After getting off the bus walk back a few steps on 18th Street to the traffic lights at 76th Avenue. Turn left and start walking east on 76th Avenue. Glenmore Square shopping centre is on the south side of 76th Avenue. The route passes River View Church on the east side of the shopping centre. East of the church is the former Ogden School building constructed in 1960 and presently occupied by a private school. On the southwest corner of 76th Avenue and 20A Street there used to be a smaller bungalow school built in 1913.

Continue east on 76th Avenue to 21A Street (0.6 km). Turn left and walk north to 74th Avenue. There are several older homes on 21st Street between 76th and 74th Avenues. Turn right on 74th Avenue and walk one block east to 22nd Street. On the north side of 74th Avenue is George Moss Park. Moss emigrated to Canada from England in 1906 settling in Calgary in 1913. He was one of the early coordinators of the Ogden-Millican Community Association serving as the association secretary for 39 years. He played an instrumental role in the creation of a recreational area so that unemployed Calgarians would have somewhere to spend their time during the Depression. The park was named in his honour in 1970. If George were alive

St. Augustine's Anglican Church

today he would probably suggest adding a wading pool or water park to the park where children could play on hot summer days.

Turn right on 22nd Street and walk one block south past some older homes on the way back to 76th Avenue (1.2 km). Turn left and walk east one block to 22A Street. On the southeast corner of the intersection is St. Augustine's Anglican Church. This 1912 church is an excellent example of the small churches first built in Calgary. Some of the larger congregations close to downtown then replaced their smaller churches with a larger building. The first page of the St. Augustine's record book in 1912 states "The first service held in this mission was last Sunday. Only 15 were present, among them three children, an Austrian who could not speak English, an intoxicated Swede, the rest being young Englishmen." St. Augustine, the son of St. Monica, was born in 354. His theological writings are very well-known. He started the Augustinian order of monks.

In 1939 when King George VI and Queen Elizabeth visited Calgary the only red carpet that could be found was some carpet ordered by St. Augustine's which was long enough to reach from the curb to the foot of the City Hall stairs. Later the carpet was laid in the church. The second building south of 76th Avenue on the west side of 22A Street across from the church is the St. Augustine's Church Hall. In 1921, the church bought this building from the City of Calgary. The building had been a restaurant built to accommodate the construction workers from the CPR shops. The building had also been used as the training headquarters for one of the adversaries

St. Augustine's church 1921. Glenbow Archives NA-2888-22

Ogden United Church – note the tower where the minister used to live.

in the ill-fated World Boxing Championship held in Calgary in 1913 when one of the boxers died as a result of a blow in the first round of the fight. This building was moved to its present site after the church was moved across the street to its present location on the corner. Water was not installed in the hall until 1957. Prior to this, water had to be hauled from the vicarage (the house on the north side of the hall) or from the Smart family residence across the alley. The photo on the previous page showed the church and the hall being moved.

From the corner head north one block on 22A Street and turn right on 74th Avenue. Walk east one block to 23rd Street. On the southwest corner is Ogden United Church. The beginning of this Ogden congregation was 1912 with the first services being held in the dining hall of the Ogden shops. The following year both the Ogden Hotel and the Picture Hall on 26th Street were used for services. In the warm weather a large tent was pitched between 73rd and 74th Avenues on 26th Street. The original church building (a structure of 50 feet by 30 feet) was erected in 1914 at a cost of $3,500 with both Presbyterian and Methodist ministers serving the congregation prior to their decision to join the United Church of Canada in June 1925. At one time the resident minister lived on the top floor of the small tower on the northeast corner of the building.

From the church cross to the north side of 74th Avenue and angle to the right across George Moss Park to the northeast corner at 72nd Avenue and 24th Street. The Ogden Cottage School was built on the present site of the skating rink in George Moss Park in 1912. In 1914 a team of horses was used to move the cottage school up the hill to 18th Street between 62nd and 64th Avenues in Millican. The building was later demolished.

Walk north on 24th Street to where it joins Ogden Road just south of 69th Avenue (1.9 km). On the east side of Ogden Road at 69th Avenue is the former Alyth Lodge (also know as Ogden Hotel), constructed in 1912. The building was constructed by the Calgary Brewery to be used as a hotel for brewery workers and Ogden Shop employees. In WWI, a Calgary veterans' hospital occupied the building. The brewery continued to operate the building from 1920 until it was purchased by the provincial government in 1935. From then until the 1970s it was used as a single men's relief hostel. A private owner then turned the building into a rooming house with the ground floor being used for retail businesses. The final transformation was in the past few years when the Victory Outreach Foundation purchased the building and made extensive upgrades. Single men can now rent a room in the impressively restored Victory Manor.

From the corner of Ogden Road and 69th Avenue walk west one block and turn right onto Crestwood Road. Follow Crestwood Road as it angles northwest. The first Ogden Fire Hall (No. 9) was located at 68th Avenue and Crestwood Road. This building was also used as a police station. Turn left off Crestwood Road on 66th Avenue (2.6 km) and walk west to 19th Street near the parking lot for Sherwood School.

You are now in the community of Millican. Banting and Best School is to the west across a parking lot from Sherwood School. The school is named for Doctor Frederick Banting who, with the assistance of Charles Best and James Collip, began studies to find a cure for diabetes. In 1922 they isolated insulin which is used to combat diabetes.

Turn right on 19th Street and walk north to the intersection of 62nd Avenue on the left and Millican Road on the right (3.4 km). There are some older homes on 19th Street between 62nd and 66th Avenues. Turn right and walk a few steps east on Millican Road to where you can observe Pop Davies Park on the right. This triangular-shaped park is at the base of the small escarpment slope on the west side of Ogden Road. The park is named for Jack "Pop" Davies who was an active community volunteer for almost thirty years. Davies also volunteered with the Boy Scouts, other youth groups and the Ogden Legion. He died in 1979.

Military hospital at Ogden, 1917. Glenbow Archives NA-3417-6

Retrace your steps back to 19th Street and 62nd Avenue and walk one block west on 62nd Avenue to 18A Street. On the northwest corner of the intersection is an older corner grocery store. Turn right and walk north on 18A Street to 59A Avenue. North of 59A Avenue is a fenced off area that is the site of one of Calgary's most serious environmental problems. A refinery site with storage tanks was located on the top of the escarpment south of the CNR tracks. The first area south of the tracks that had to be reclaimed was at the base of the escarpment within the boundaries of present-day Beaverdam Flats Park. The area from 59A Avenue north to the tracks had been developed into a residential area with single-family homes and several apartment buildings. As the seriousness of the leakage from the old tanks became evident all but a few homes backing on the escarpment had to be demolished. At the present time the area remains fenced off with an uncertain future use.

Walk west one block on 59A Avenue and turn left heading south on 18th Street back to 62nd Avenue. West of 17A Street and 18th Street one of the large green spaces in the community extends south from 59A Avenue to 66th Avenue. Turn left at 62nd Avenue and then right on 18th Street walking south

Mural on the north side of Millican Ogden Community Hall

past some older homes back to 66th Avenue.

Turn left and walk east along 66th Avenue and turn right on the sidewalk beside Banting and Best School on the west side of the parking lot between the two schools. From the south side of the parking lot head south across the playing fields to 69th Avenue (5.1 km) passing by the west side of the collection of buildings at the south side of this large open green space. The most westerly building is the Jack Setters Arena built in 1976 and named for long-time hockey volunteer, Jack Setters. He worked with Rose Kohn and Stu Peppard to restructure minor hockey in Calgary in the early 1960s. Setters also served as president of the Minor Hockey Association. For his years of hard work he was honoured as the Calgary Booster Club Sportsman of the Year in 1972. The arena is now owned and operated by the community association. Two other arenas in Calgary have been named for Rose Kohn and Stu Peppard.

Walk east on 69th Avenue past the other buildings. The Millican-Ogden Outdoor Swimming Pool is beside the arena. Next to the pool is the Ogden House Seniors Building. The final building beside 20A Street is the Millican

Ogden Community Association (MOCA) hall. There is a mural on the north wall of the community hall.

Retrace your steps back along 69th Avenue and turn left into a long thin park that stretches south to an escarpment slope. A plaque on a rock identifies this park as Harry Huish Park. Huish, a long-time resident of Calgary, served as a city alderman from 1974 to 1980. As you walk south through the park note the rather straight lines of large trees planted in a north-south alignment in the park.

At the south end of the park at the top of the escarpment, angle to the right and wander across the slope to reach 18th Street. Turn left and follow 18th Street south down the hill to the intersection with 76th Avenue. Cross to the southwest corner of the intersection and walk a few steps south to the bus stop (6.3 km).

Bus Directions from the end of the route to the station:

Catch bus # 41 Riverbend at stop 6132 on the southwest corner of 18th Street and 76th Avenue (5.9 km). The scheduled time back to the station is 8 minutes. The bus frequency is 45 minutes daily. Get off at stop 6451 back at the station. During the construction of the station the bus will use the temporary stop 4439 on 3rd Street between 59th and 60th Avenues.

Route Summary:

1. Catch bus # 41 Lynnwood and get off at the stop on northbound 18th Street just north of 76th Avenue.
2. After getting off the bus walk a few steps back to the traffic lights at 18th Street and 76th Avenue.
3. Turn left and walk east on 76th Avenue to 21A Street.
4. Turn left and walk north on 21A Street to 74th Avenue.
5. Turn right and walk east on 74th Avenue and turn right on 22nd Street.
6. Walk south back to 76th Avenue and turn left.
7. Walk east one block on 76th Avenue and turn left at 22A Street.
8. Walk north on 22A Street and turn right on 74th Avenue walking one block to 23rd Street.
9. Cross to the north side of 74th Avenue at 23rd Street.
10. Angle to the right across George Moss Park to 72nd Avenue and 24th Street.
11. Walk north on 24th Street and turn left on Ogden Road to 69th Avenue.
12. Turn left and walk west on 69th Avenue turning right on Crestwood Road.
13. Follow Crestwood Road and turn left on 66th Avenue.
14. Walk west on 66th Avenue and turn right on 19th Street.
15. Walk north on 19th Street and walk a few steps east on Millican Road.
16. Retrace your steps and walk west on 62nd Avenue turning right on 18A Street.

17. Walk north on 18A Street and turn left on 59A Avenue.
18. Walk west to the next corner and turn left walking south on 18th Street back to 62nd Avenue.
19. Turn left on 62nd Avenue and turn right on 18A Street walking back to 66th Avenue.
20. Turn left and walk east to the sidewalk on the east side of Banting and Best School.
21. Turn right on the sidewalk and cross the field to 69th Avenue on the west side of Jack Setters Arena.
22. Turn left and walk east on 69th Avenue to 20A Street.
23. Retrace your steps and turn left into Harry Huish Park.
24. Walk to the south end of the park at the top of the escarpment slope.
25. Turn right and angle across the slope to 18th Street.
26. Turn left and walk down the hill to 76th Avenue.
27. Cross to the southwest corner and catch bus # 36 Riverbend.

Chapter Five
Heritage Station

Station Information: The station is on the south side of Heritage Drive just west of Macleod Trail on the north end of Haysboro Industrial area. Haysboro community is west of the station, Kingsland community is north of the station and Acadia community is east across Macleod Trail. The land for the communities of Haysboro, Kingsland and Acadia was annexed in 1956. Haysboro is situated on land once owned by Harry Hays, who served politically as Calgary mayor, a Member of Parliament and a Canadian senator. Development of Kingsland started in 1957 followed by Haysboro in 1958 and Acadia in 1960.

Stairs and an up escalator at the north end of the station connect the centre platform to the + 15 level of the station. Handicapped access to the platform is at a ground level track crossing at the south end of the park and ride lot. There are plaques at the upper level of the station with information about the 1909 streetcars and about streetcars in Calgary between 1909 and 1950.

Heritage Walk 1
East Glenmore Park &
Heritage Town Square

Walk Overview: The route starts on 90th Avenue at 16th Street SW. From here it heads north on the west side of Glenmore Landing shopping centre and continues north at the east end of Glenmore Reservoir. The route passes by the entrance to Heritage Park and Heritage Town Square before entering the community of Eagle Ridge. On the north side of this community the route passes by the west side of Rockyview General Hospital and Carewest Glenmore Park. At the overpass across Glenmore Trail retrace your steps back to Heritage Town Square. The final location on the route is the Bissett Wetlands Heritage Wetland Walk.

Length: 5.6 km

Route Description & Accessibility: This relatively flat route has good accessibility with a few short ascents/descents north of Heritage Park.

The walking surface for most of the route is paved paths or asphalt on a road with no sidewalks. The trail around Bissett Wetlands is less accessible.

Food and Drink: There are several options at Glenmore Landing with a grocery, several restaurants, a coffee shop and a bakery. Heritage Town Square near the entrance to Heritage Park has a café in a replica railway station.

Washrooms: There are no public washrooms on this route.

Map References: Clear-View – 48 & 42, MapArt – 174
Rand McNally – 66, Sherlock – 40

Route Category: Bus/Walk/Bus – Ride the bus to the start of the route and when the walk is finished ride the bus back to the station.

Bus Directions from the station to the start of the walk:

Catch bus # 80 Oakridge/Acadia at stop 5762 at the station. Get off at stop 4232 on westbound 90th Avenue at 16th Street. This stop is 8 minutes from the station. The bus frequency is 35 minutes at mid-day on weekdays and 30 minutes on Saturdays and Sundays.

View of Heritage Park from East Glenmore Park

The Walk: After getting off the bus walk to the traffic lights on 90th Avenue at 16th Street. Follow a path heading north past the east side of the community of Bayview. This community along with the adjacent communities of Pump Hill and Palliser was developed in the late 1960s.

At the first junction take the left branch as the right branch leads to Glenmore Landing. A three-way junction with the east-west path along the south side of the Glenmore Reservoir is just past the first junction. Take the centre path. The right branch at this junction also goes to Glenmore Landing and the left branch heads west along the south side of the reservoir. In a couple more steps there is another junction (0.2 km). The left branch joins the path along the south side of the reservoir. Continue straight ahead on the path that heads north along the east side of the reservoir. From this section of path there is a good view to the west across the reservoir. The path soon reaches the large letter "H" for Heritage Park (0.9 km). Nearby there is an information plaque about the area. The path then turns left along the south side of the Heritage Park access road. After passing an angle parking area turn right and cross over the access road. On the right is a large parking lot and on the left are the buildings in the Heritage Town Square

Replicas of historic billboards at Heritage Town Square

section of Heritage Park. You will visit this area on the return portion of the walk. The next walk in this chapter visits Heritage Park. There is an admission charge for Heritage Park. Information on Heritage Park is included in the description of the next walk.

The path crosses a second access road and then crosses the park's streetcar tracks. Of interest on the left are the outside walls of Gasoline Alley Museum with large billboards replicating some early billboards. The route then passes between houses in the Eagle Ridge community and turns left on Eagle Ridge Drive (1.5 km). Eagle Ridge, one of Calgary's smallest communities, was established in 1960.

This northbound section of Eagle Ridge Drive has a slight ascent. There are no sidewalks so use caution. Continue on Eagle Ridge Drive as it turns right and goes down a slight descent. Look for a path between houses on the left (1.8 km). Follow this path through an undeveloped area on the north side of Eagle Ridge.

Within a short distance the route passes the west side of Rockyview General Hospital. The hospital is aptly named as there is a great view of the Rocky Mountains from the top of the escarpment overlooking the Glenmore Reservoir. The path then enters a treed area with several turns and blind corners and some small ascents/descents. Keep to the right to avoid collisions with cyclists. The path leaves the treed area as it reaches a junction overlooking Glenmore Trail from the south side. This is the turn around point on this route (2.8 km). The left branch at the junction follows the sidewalk across an overpass to the north side of Glenmore Trail. From there the path crosses the Glenmore Dam to reach the turn around point for the 39th Avenue Walk 2 – Stanley Park, River Park and Sandy Beach.

From the turn around point retrace the route back to Heritage Town Square. An excellent collection of information plaques is scattered throughout Heritage Town Square. In the Haskayne Mercantile Block visitors have the opportunity to make a purchase from a wide variety of historically themed merchandise. Next to that building is the replica Calgary Public Market building housing the Gasoline Alley Museum and the Selkirk Grille. Continuing counterclockwise around the edge of the square there is a small building where visitors can buy admission tickets to the park.

The next building houses the Railway Café in a replica railway station. A plaque describes the first Calgary CPR station built in 1893 and replaced by a larger station in 1911. At one time at least two westbound passenger trains to Vancouver and two eastbound passenger trains to Toronto passed through Calgary every day. The only passenger train service now operating in Calgary is the Rocky Mountaineer train between Calgary and Vancouver.

Pathway north of the Rockyview General Hospital

Replica railway station at Heritage Town Square

Beside the railway station is a recreated railway gardens area. Starting in the 1890s many station agents planted flower gardens to beautify the area around their station. Most of these gardens had disappeared by the 1950s. Perhaps gardens could be recreated at each of the LRT stations. Before leaving the Heritage Town Square you may want to stop at the Railway Café.

From here retrace your route back to the letter "H" beside the Heritage Park access road. There is one more area to visit before catching the bus back to the station. Cross over the Heritage Park access road and walk past the waiting area for the streetcar ride that takes park visitors to the gates of Heritage Park. On the north side of this waiting area is Bissett Wetlands Heritage Wetland Walk (4.8 km), an interesting area created by the efforts of philanthropists Leslie and David Bissett. A short stroll around the edge of the wetlands is a nice way to finish this walk. Take the time to read numerous information plaques explaining the importance of water on the prairies.

From the wetlands walk east to 14th Street and cross to the southeast corner of Heritage Drive and 14th Street. Walk a short distance east to catch

Bissett Wetlands at 14th Street and Heritage Drive

the bus back to the station (5.6 km).

Bus Directions from the end of the route back to the station: You have the choice of catching either bus # 20 Heritage or bus # 79 Acadia at stop 5761 on eastbound Heritage Drive at Haysboro Crescent. Get off at stop 5762 for bus # 20 and stop 6412 for bus # 79. Stop 5761 is 4 minutes from the station. The bus frequency for bus # 20 is 20 minutes at mid-day on weekdays and 30 minutes on Saturdays and Sundays. The bus frequency for bus # 79 is 35 minutes at mid-day on weekdays and 30 minutes on Saturdays and Sundays. An option is to walk 1.2 km east along Heritage Drive back to the station.

Route Summary:

1. Catch bus # 80 Oakridge and get off at the stop on westbound 90th Avenue at 16th Street.
2. Walk to the traffic lights at 90th Avenue and 16th Street and turn north on the path on the east side of the community of Bayview.
3. Walk past the path on the south side of the reservoir and continue north along the east side of the reservoir.
4. Just past the letter "H" the path turns left along the south side of the Heritage Park access road.
5. The path turns right, crosses the access road and then passes by a large parking lot.
6. The path crosses another access road and the streetcar tracks before entering a green space.
7. The path goes between houses and ends at Eagle Ridge Drive.
8. Turn left and follow Eagle Ridge Drive north and east turning left onto another path between houses.
9. The path passes by the west side of Rockyview General Hospital.
10. The path then enters a treed area with turns and some blind corners.
11. The turn around point is at a trail junction overlooking Glenmore Trail.
12. Retrace the route back to Heritage Town Square.
13. Walk back to the letter "H", cross over the Heritage Park access road and follow the trail around the Bissett Wetlands.
14. Walk east to 14th Street and cross to the southeast corner.
15. Walk east a short distance to catch either bus # 20 Heritage or bus # 79 Acadia back to the station.

Heritage Walk 2
Heritage Park

Walk Overview: A donation from the J.H. Woods Foundation assisted by a city donation of land and funds helped with the development of Heritage Park. Almost fifty years after opening in 1965, Heritage Park continues to evolve as more buildings are added. It may require more than one visit to view everything. The route length is not included for this walk. Do your own off-route exploring based on personal interests. There is an admission charge to enter Heritage Park.

Length: N/A

Route Description & Accessibility: This route is relatively flat although there is a slight ascent/descent near the entrance gates to the park.

Food and Drink: Heritage Park has several locations where you can buy food.

Washrooms: There are several washroom facilities in the park.

Map References: Clear-View – 42, MapArt – 174
Rand McNally – 66, Sherlock – 40

Route Category: Bus/Walk/Bus – Ride the bus to the start of the route and when finished the walk ride the bus back to the station.

Bus Directions from the station to the start of the walk:
Catch bus # 20 Northmount or bus # 80 Oakridge to stop 4578 on westbound Heritage Drive near Churchill Drive. Bus # 20 leaves from stop 5762 at the station. Bus # 80 leaves from stop 5761 at the station. Stop 4578 is 4 minutes from station. The bus frequency for bus # 20 is 20 minutes at mid-day on weekdays and 30 minutes on Saturdays and Sundays. The bus frequency for bus # 80 is 35 minutes at mid-day on weekdays and on Sundays and 30 minutes on Saturdays.

The Walk: After getting off the bus walk west along Heritage Drive and cross to the west side of 14th Street. From here there are two options to reach the park gates. On the north side of the access road west of 14th Street you can catch a streetcar up the hill to the park gates. The streetcar is about 0.3 km from the bus stop. The second choice is to cross to the south side of the access road and follow the path on the south side of the access road up to the park gates. It is about 0.9 km from the bus stop to the building where you buy your tickets. This building is located behind the Railway Café building.

A street scene in Heritage Park

The park is a mixture of original and replica buildings with some dating back to pre-1914. The buildings are arranged along several streets, giving visitors the atmosphere of strolling through a prairie village almost 100 years ago. You can take a ride on a paddlewheel boat on the Glenmore Reservoir or ride the historic train as it circles around the park stopping at several stations. There is an amusement park with old-fashioned rides for children. A ride on a horse-drawn wagon can also be included in the visit. After wandering around the park for several hours, visitors can stop at one of the park's restaurants or concessions. After visiting the park walk back down the access road to 14th Street and Heritage Drive. The bus stop is on the south side of Heritage Drive a short distance east of 14th Street.

Bus Directions from the end of the route back to the station:
Catch either bus # 20 Heritage or bus # 79 Acadia at stop 5761 on eastbound Heritage Drive at Haysboro Crescent. Get off at the station at stop 5762 for bus # 20 and stop 6412 for bus # 79. Stop 5761 is 4 minutes from the station. The bus frequency for bus # 20 is 20 minutes at mid-day on weekdays and 30 minutes on Saturdays and Sundays. The bus frequency for bus # 79 is 35 minutes at mid-day on weekdays and 30 minutes on Saturdays and Sundays. Another option is to walk 1.2 km east along Heritage Drive back to the station.

Heritage Park

Route Summary:

1. Catch bus # 20 Northmount or bus # 80 Oakridge and get off at the stop on westbound Heritage Drive near Churchill Drive.
2. Walk west on Heritage Drive to 14th Street and cross to the northwest corner of the intersection.
3. From here catch the Heritage Park streetcar up to the park gates or follow the path on the south side of the access road up a gradual ascent to the park gates.
4. When leaving the park retrace your route by either catching the streetcar back to 14th Street or following the path back to 14th Street.
5. Cross to the southeast corner and walk a few steps east on Heritage Drive. Catch bus # 20 Heritage or bus # 79 Acadia back to the station. Another option is to walk 1.2 km east along Heritage Drive back to the station.

Heritage Walk 3
Weaselhead Flats Natural Area

Walk Overview: The walk follows an out-and-back route on a path along the top of the escarpment in South Glenmore Park starting near the northwest corner of Oakridge. The path leads down an escarpment slope into Weaselhead Flats Natural Area and continues on the flats to a pedestrian bridge across the Elbow River. Those wanting to explore the forested river valley can then follow some trails on a linear route before rejoining the path just before climbing back up the escarpment. Weaselhead Flats is about 237 hectares in size. It is situated between North Glenmore Park on top of the escarpment on the north side of the Elbow River beside the community of Lakeview, and South Glenmore Park on the top of the escarpment on the south side of the Elbow River beside the community of Oakridge. A point of interest is that Calgary's only delta is in Weaselhead Flats. The delta started forming in the 1930s after Glenmore Dam was built.

There are two possible opinions re: the origin of the name Weaselhead with the more popular and most likely being that Weaselhead was a Tsuu T'ina chief living nearby when the first Europeans travelled through the area. A less popular suggestion is that the name was given to one of the Tsuu T'ina chiefs by a European. The name Glenmore (Gaelic for *Big Valley*) comes from the name Sam Livingston gave to his farm. His homestead was located near the east end of the valley in the area now covered by water after the Glenmore Dam was built. You can see his original house in Heritage Park. Most of this route is isolated so use your own discretion about walking alone.

Length: 9.3 km

Route Description & Accessibility: The accessibility is only good until you reach the long steep descent into the river valley. On the return portion of the walk you ascend the same hill. No alternate route to reach Weaselhead Flats Natural Area is included in the text. The trails leading off the paved path in the river valley are uneven and can be wet or muddy.

Food and Drink: There are no stores or restaurants along this route.

Washrooms: There are washrooms in a building next to a city equipment storage yard on the north side of 90th Avenue near Oakmount Drive.

Map References: Clear-View – 47 & 41, MapArt – 173
Rand McNally – 65, Sherlock – 40 & 39

Route Category: Bus/Walk/Bus – Ride the bus to the start of the route and when finished the walk ride the bus back to the station.

Path west of 90th Avenue and Oakmount Drive

Bus Directions from the station to the start of the walk:

Catch bus # 80 Oakridge at stop 5762 at the station. Get off at stop 6434 on southbound Palliser Drive just south of 90th Avenue. This stop is 14 minutes from the station. The bus frequency is 35 minutes at mid-day on weekdays and 30 minutes on Saturdays and Sundays.

The Walk: After getting off the bus walk back to 90th Avenue and turn left walking west to the corner of 90th Avenue and Oakmount Drive. Cross to the north side of 90th Avenue and follow a path that passes by the east side of a parking lot (0.3 km). On the west side of the parking lot is a City of Calgary building that includes public washrooms. A second path from the parking lot joins your path after a few steps. Within a short distance the path reaches the main east-west path that passes through both South Glenmore Park and Weaselhead Flats Natural Area (0.6 km).

Turn left on this main path and begin following it west. There are several information plaques along the path. Stay on the main path going right at a junction where the path along the west side of Oakridge joins your path. Southland Walk 1 – Palliser, Oakridge & South Glenmore Park has a short section of the route on this path. The treed area the route passes through on the top of the escarpment does restrict the view to the north. The route then descends the slope to the river valley crossing a small bridge (2.5 km) and going past a pond. The path then makes a sharp turn to the right and starts heading in a northeasterly direction. Continue straight ahead at a junction with a trail on the left. That trail is on the return route. Continue along the path ignoring any trails leading left or right. The path leads to a pedestrian bridge across the Elbow River (4.0 km). There are also information plaques on the near side of the bridge. On the Chinook Walk 1 – North Glenmore Park the turn around point is on the other side of this bridge.

From the bridge there are two options. The first choice is to retrace the route back along the paved path, climbing the hill and continuing along the top of the escarpment back to 90th Avenue. Cross to the south side of 90th Avenue and walk east to stop 6427 and catch bus # 79 Acadia back to the station (8.0 km).

The second option is to explore some of the trails on the floodplain in Weaselhead Flats. From the bridge retrace the route a few steps and turn right onto a trail leading over a second bridge that crosses an old river channel. On the far side of the bridge turn right at the junction as the trail continues close to the river. At an open area, stay on the main trail. The route reaches a sign about military activity. The area was used for training by the military in the early 1900s. Look for evidence of where they dug foxholes.

The route then reaches a junction near a sign about the Elbow River (4.8 km). The trail to the right soon ends as that area was eroded by the high waters of the river in the 2005 flooding. Take the left trail from the junction. At the next major junction follow the right branch. The left branch leads back to the second bridge you crossed at the start of the trail.

The trail on the right soon leads to another junction. From here there is another option. The left branch is just a short distance from the paved path. You could take that trail and turn right on the path retracing your steps back to the bus stop. The right branch continues through the forest crossing a boardwalk that passes over an old river channel. Shortly after that, you finish your exploration of the trails through the forest when the trail joins the paved path (6.4 km). Turn right and follow the path making the sharp turn around the pond, crossing the small bridge at the bottom of the escarpment and climbing the slope. Follow the path back along the top of the escarpment to where you first joined the main path. Turn right and walk past the parking lot to 90th Avenue. Cross to the south side of 90th Avenue, turn left and walk east past Palliser Drive to the bus stop (9.3 km).

Bus Directions from the end of the route back to the station: Catch bus # 79 Acadia at stop 6427 on 90th Avenue at Palliser Drive. Get off at stop 6412 at the station. The stop is 15 minutes from the station. The bus frequency is 35 minutes at mid-day on weekdays and 30 minutes on Saturdays and Sundays.

Route Summary:

1. Catch bus # 80 Oakridge and get off at the stop on southbound Palliser Drive just south of 90th Avenue.
2. Walk back to 90th Avenue and turn left walking west to the corner of 90th Avenue and Oakmount Drive.
3. Cross to the north side of 90th Avenue and follow a path passing by the east side of a parking lot.
4. Within a short distance the path reaches the main east-west path.
5. Turn left and follow the main path staying right at a junction in the first 200 metres.
6. Use caution going down a long downhill section where you cross a bridge at the bottom of the slope.
7. Make a sharp right turn and follow the path all the way to a bridge over the Elbow River.
8. From the bridge retrace the route for a few steps and turn right on a trail that crosses another bridge.
9. At a junction beyond the bridge follow the right branch.
10. When you reach a junction near a sign about the Elbow River take the left branch.
11. At the next junction take the right branch. The left branch leads back to the second bridge.
12. At the following junction again take the right branch. The left branch leads back to the nearby paved path.
13. The trail crosses a boardwalk over an old river channel.
14. The trail soon returns to the paved path.
15. Turn right and retrace your steps back to 90th Avenue and Palliser Drive.
16. Catch bus # 79 Acadia on 90th Avenue just east of Palliser Drive.

Chapter Six
Southland Station

Station Information: The station is on the south side of Southland Drive just east of Sacramento Drive. Southwood community is west of the station and Willow Park community is east of the station. Southwood was developed in the late 1950s. The area occupied by Willow Park was annexed in 1956 with development starting almost ten years later. Stairs and an up escalator at the north end of the station platform connect to the upper level of the station building. Handicapped access to the platform is at a track crossing at the south end of the park and ride lot. Two plaques at the upper level of the station provide details about the trolley buses that started operating in Calgary in 1947 and the diesel buses used from 1960 to 1970.

Southland Walk 1
Palliser, Oakridge &
South Glenmore Park

Walk Overview: From Southland Leisure Centre this route follows a path west through Oakridge to the north-south path on the west side of Oakridge and Cedarbrae. The route then heads north into South Glenmore Park. The route leaves South Glenmore Park near the Glenmore Landing Shopping Centre and wanders through the community of Pump Hill. The area that is Pump Hill was formerly named Strawberry Hill. Thomas Patton drilled a well on his homestead in this area in 1910. For many years Patton's windmill was also on this site. The windmill was donated to Fort Calgary and is now located in the garden behind the Fort. There was an earlier pump than Patton's on the top of the hill. The community name is derived from this earlier pump.

In 1956 the city annexed the area south of Glenmore Reservoir. The Palliser community north of the leisure centre and the communities of Bayview and Pump Hill were established in 1967. The community of Oakridge was established the following year. Palliser is named for Captain John Palliser. From 1857 to 1860 John Palliser led a scientific expedition through Western Canada exploring the area from Cypress Hills to the Rocky Mountains. From his explorations, Palliser came to the conclusion that very little would grow in southwest Saskatchewan and southeast Alberta, an area that came to be known as *Palliser's Triangle*. The land around the Glenmore Reservoir was set aside for park use in the mid 1950s.

Length: 9.2 km

Route Description & Accessibility: Most of this relatively flat linear walk has good accessibility. There is one short descent in South Glenmore Park. Most of the route has a walking surface of paved paths or sidewalks with one short section on grass in Pump Hill.

Food and Drink: South Glenmore Park has a picnic area. Southland Leisure Centre has a food concession. Later in the route you pass the Glenmore Landing Shopping Centre with a grocery store, a coffee shop, restaurants and a bakery.

Washrooms: There are washrooms at Southland Leisure Centre at the start of the walk. Along the route there are washrooms north of 90th Avenue at Oakmount Drive in a building next to a city equipment storage yard. There are also washrooms in South Glenmore Park north of 90th Avenue and 24th Street near the Glenmore Sailing Club.

Map References: Clear-View – 47 & 48, MapArt – 184, 183, 173 & 174 Rand McNally – 74 & 73, Sherlock – 40 & 39

Route Category: Bus/Walk/Bus – Ride the bus to the start of the route and when finished the walk ride the bus back to the station.

Bus Directions from the station to the start of the walk: Catch bus # 56 Woodbine at stop 6097 at the station. Get off at stop 9178 on westbound Southland Drive near 19th Street. This stop is 6 minutes from the station. The bus frequency is 30 minutes daily at mid-day.

The Walk: Walk north along the east side of Southland Leisure Centre parking lot. St. Benedict School is on the right. Born in 480 CE into a family of Roman nobility, Benedict decided to live a holy life by establishing his home in a cave.

The route reaches a path leading north. On the left is Tom Brook Athletic Park. Brook was a strong supporter of sports in Calgary and served as president of the Calgary Stampeders Football Club. In 1975 he was inducted into the Canadian Football Hall of Fame. Brook also provided monetary support for the development of this park located on land he once owned. The two arenas in Southland Leisure Centre are named for two well-known Calgarians. Ed Whalen worked for many years in the broadcast industry as a sportscaster and as a radio/television personality. Joe Kryzcka was a strong volunteer supporter of hockey in Calgary.

On the right before the route reaches 98th Avenue is John Ware School. After being freed from slavery at the end of the American Civil War, John Ware worked on a cattle drive that headed north from Texas to Idaho. He then joined another cattle drive that ended in High River. Within a short time he had established his own cattle ranch, moving to an area near the Red Deer River. There is a building on the SAIT campus named for John Ware. In February 2012 Canada Post issued a commemorative stamp to honour John Ware.

At the corner of 98th Avenue and 19th Street (0.3 km) turn left and start walking west along the sidewalk towards 24th Street. The dividing line between the communities of Palliser and Pump Hill is 19th Street extending north from 98th Avenue to 90th Avenue. On the left from Tom Brook Park to 24th Street the route passes several multi-unit housing complexes.

Use caution crossing 24th Street at 98th Avenue (1.3 km) as there is no pedestrian crossing light or traffic light. Continue straight ahead to where 98th Avenue soon ends and a path starts. Follow this path west. The path crosses 26th Street and continues westbound through a green space between houses (1.6 km). There is a large playing field area on the left just before Oakfield Drive (2.3 km). The path continues westbound until it reaches a T-intersection on the west side of Oakridge (2.8 km). Turn right at this junction and begin walking north. The path to the left at the T-intersection leads south along the west side of Cedarbrae. After crossing

Path through Oakridge west of 26th Street

South Glenmore Park just west of the Sailing Club

Anderson Road at 37th Street that path continues south along the west side of Woodbine into the Shannon Terrace area of Fish Creek Park.

On the left as you head north is the east boundary fence of the Tsuu T'ina Reserve. Near the northwest corner of Oakridge the path angles to the right before joining the main east-west path through Weaselhead Park Natural Area and South Glenmore Park (4.7 km). The area west of Oakridge could change if 90th Avenue is ever extended west to connect with the southwest ring road.

This next short section on the main path is also on the route for Heritage Walk 3 – Weaselhead Natural Area. At the next junction take the left branch or the main path along the top of the escarpment above Glenmore Reservoir. The right branch leads to a building with washrooms next to a city equipment storage yard. That section of path is at the start and end of the Heritage Walk 3 – Weaselhead Flats Natural Area.

There is a trail that extends along the escarpment slope called the Jackrabbit Trail. However, this trail with numerous ascents/descents can be a bit overgrown in some places.

Path along the south side of Glenmore Reservoir north of Bayview

Near the north end of 24th Street the path splits. Take the left branch that stays closer to the top of the escarpment. The right branch is for cyclists to bypass the very busy area around a children's water park, some picnic tables and a playground. The two branches join on the west side of the access road to the Glenmore Sailing Club (6.0 km). The access road starts at the intersection of 24th Street and 90th Avenue.

From the access road there are two route options. The path to the left on the east side of the access road goes down a short descent and then travels along the edge of the Glenmore Reservoir. On this path there are a few turns with limited visibility so keep to the right as this path is shared with cyclists. This section of path is a bit isolated so use your own discretion about walking alone. The path may also be icy in the winter as it receives very little sun. There are good views of the reservoir, North Glenmore Park and Heritage Park from the path.

The path to the right from the east side of the access road stays on top of the escarpment passing through a treed area on the north side of Bayview. As the left path from the access road nears the west side of Glenmore Landing shopping centre the path along the top of the escarpment joins the route. At the junction by the shopping centre turn right and head south on a path to 90th Avenue (7.9 km). This section of path is also on the route for Heritage Walk 1 – East Glenmore Park and Heritage Town Square.

At 90th Avenue cross to the south side of the road at the traffic lights and continue straight ahead on Jerusalem Road or 16th Street. This road leads past the Calgary Jewish Centre. There is a small park area in front of the centre with the focal point in the park being a memorial to the victims of the Holocaust.

At the next corner where Jerusalem Road or 16th Street meets 92nd Avenue turn right and follow 92nd Avenue to where it ends in a cul-de-sac (8.5 km). Walk past a barrier separating 92nd Avenue from Pump Hill Way on the left. Turn left and walk south on Pump Hill Way. At the next corner take the left branch onto 300 Pump Hill Gardens. When the road ends continue south through a green space to reach the location where 96th Avenue turns left and becomes Pump Hill Drive. Turn right and follow the road a few steps to reach Palliser Drive (9.0 km). Please note that some of the roads in Pump Hill have no sidewalk. Cross to the far side of Palliser Drive and turn left walking south to the nearest bus stop near Pump Hill Rise (9.2 km).

Bus Directions from the end of the route to the station:
Catch bus # 84 Palliser at stop 4649 on southbound Palliser Drive. Get off at stop 5624 back to the station. This stop is 6 or 7 minutes from the station. The bus frequency is 40 minutes at mid-day on weekdays and 30 minutes on Saturday and Sunday.

Route Summary:
1. Catch bus # 56 Woodbine and get off at the stop on westbound Southland Drive near 19th Street.
2. Walk north along the east side of the leisure centre parking lot.
3. From the parking lot a path leads north to 98th Avenue and 19th Street.
4. Turn left and walk west on 98th Avenue.
5. Cross 24th Street and continue west on 98th Avenue to where the road ends and a path begins.
6. Follow the path west crossing 26th Street.
7. Continue on the path crossing Oakfield Drive.
8. The path continues west to a T-intersection.
9. Turn right and follow the path north on the west side of Oakridge.
10. The path angles to the right and joins the main east-west path through South Glenmore Park.
11. At a junction north of a city building continue straight ahead.
12. At the next junction again stay left.
13. When the path reaches the sailing club access road there are two paths leading away from the east side of the road. Take the left path down a

small descent and along the edge of the Glenmore Reservoir.

14. The right path stays on top of the escarpment along the north side of Bayview. These two paths join just west of Glenmore Landing shopping centre.
15. At the pathway junction by the shopping centre turn right and follow a path south on the east side of Bayview to reach 90th Avenue.
16. Cross 90th Avenue and head south on 16th Street (Jerusalem Road) to 92nd Avenue.
17. Turn right and walk west to where 92nd Avenue ends by a barrier.
18. Pass the barrier and turn left walking south on Pump Hill Way.
19. At the next corner take the left branch walking south to the end of 300 Pump Hill Gardens.
20. Walk south through a green space to where 96th Avenue meets Pump Hill Drive.
21. Turn right and walk a short distance to Palliser Drive.
22. Cross to the west side of Palliser Drive, turn left and walk south to the nearest bus stop by Pump Hill Rise.
23. Catch bus # 84 Palliser back to the station.

Chapter Seven
Anderson Station

Station Information: The station is on the west side of Macleod Trail just south of 109th Avenue. Southwood community is west of the station and Willow Park community and Southcentre Mall are east across Macleod Trail from the station. Southwood developed in the late 1950s. At the north end of the centre platform there is a ground level crossing of the tracks to the park and ride lot. Use caution crossing the tracks. At the south end of the platform, stairs and an up escalator connect to the upper level of the station. A left turn at the upper level leads to stairs down to the ground level for buses and parking. The other option for the left turn at the upper level is access to a pedestrian overpass across Macleod Trail. A right turn at the upper level provides access to an overpass leading down into a park area in the southeast corner of Southwood. At the upper level a plaque provides details about the origins of light rail transit in Calgary. Anderson Road south of the station is named for Harry T. Anderson. He farmed a quarter section of land in this area from 1913 to 1960. All three walks described in this chapter require a bus ride to the start of the route and a bus ride back to the station from the end of the route.

Anderson Walk 1
Woodbine & Woodlands

Walk Overview: Most of this linear route follows the escarpment on the north side of Fish Creek Park along the southern edge of the communities of Woodbine and Woodlands. There are good views from this south-facing escarpment slope. Woodlands and Woodbine were both developed in the 1980s.

Length: 5.4 km

Route Description & Accessibility: Only portions of the route have good accessibility. There are some stairs to negotiate in Woodbine and a long descent in the Bebo Grove area of Fish Creek Park followed by an ascent of the escarpment slope on a trail that is very uneven and somewhat eroded. An alternate route to avoid the stairs and the descent/ascent near Bebo Grove is included in the text. The walking surface is a mix of sidewalks, paved paths and trails.

Food and Drink: Both Shannon Terrace and Bebo Grove areas in Fish Creek Park have numerous picnic tables.

Washrooms: There are public washrooms at Shannon Terrace and Bebo Grove.

Map References: Clear-View – 53, MapArt – 183 & 184
Rand McNally – 81, Sherlock – 46

Route Category: Bus/Walk/Bus – Ride the bus to the start of the route and when finished the walk ride the bus back to the station.

Bus Directions from the station to the start of the walk: Catch bus # 56 Woodbine at stop 6461. Get off at stop 9111 on westbound Woodfield Road near Woodhaven Crescent on the left. This stop is 13 minutes from the station. The bus frequency is 30 minutes daily at mid-day.

The Walk: After getting off the bus walk in the same direction as the bus route and turn left onto Woodhaven Bay (0.4 km). At a T-intersection with Woodhaven Crescent, continue straight ahead on a path between houses (0.6 km). When this path turns left behind the houses on Woodhaven Crescent you are at the top of the escarpment along the edge of Fish Creek Park overlooking the Shannon Terrace area of the park.

Shannon Terrace is named for James Shannon. He settled in this area in 1882, raising cattle on his 550 hectares ranch known as the Diamond. There are several information plaques at the bottom of the escarpment adjacent to Woodpath Road (the access road into the Shannon Terrace area of the park). Fish Creek-Lacombe Walk 1 – Evergreen Bluffs to Fish Creek-Lacombe Station Walk passes by the plaques. A riding stable with barn and corrals to the east of the access road at the bottom of the escarpment was torn down a few years ago.

Head east along the path behind the houses. There are excellent views from this path. Near the last house on the left there is a junction with a trail leading to the right down to the Shannon Terrace area. The path turns left past the side of this last house and ends at a sidewalk on Woodhaven Crescent (1.2 km). Follow the sidewalk to the right and turn right onto a trail before the sidewalk reaches Woodfield Road.

You will need to detour at the start of this trail if you require better accessibility than the trail and the escarpment slope by Bebo Grove. The detour stays on the sidewalk. At Woodfield Road turn right and follow Woodfield Road to Woodpark Boulevard. Turn right and follow Woodpark Boulevard east to 24th Street. Turn right and walk south on 24th Street. The detour rejoins the route when you turn left onto the path along the top of the escarpment east of 24th Street.

The trail on the right from the sidewalk on Woodhaven Crescent leads

View looking east from path by Woodhaven Crescent

down into a shallow gully behind the houses on Woodhaven View. There are a few stairs along this trail. When the trail ends at Woodacres Drive turn right and head south on the sidewalk (1.8 km). Look for a path on your left between houses. This path leads down the slope into the Bebo Grove area of Fish Creek Park. Stay left at the two junctions on this path. At the bottom of the slope there is a washroom building beside the Bebo Grove parking lot (2.5 km).

Nelson Bebo squatted on the land that is now Bebo Grove from 1888 until 1899. He farmed and hauled wood from the Tsuu T'ina land west of this location. Addison Hone, a wealthy settler from Ireland and a dedicated polo player, then purchased the land in 1905. Teams would compete for the Hone Cup at the Fish Creek polo grounds east of the parking lot. A stone fireplace and chimney adjacent to the washroom building are all that remains of a home that was located in this area. Fish Creek-Lacombe Walk 1 Evergreen Bluffs to Fish Creek/Lacombe Station also passes through the Bebo Grove area.

The path down the escarpment ends at 24th Street (the access road into Bebo Grove). At this point turn left and follow a trail up the slope on the west side of 24th Street. This trail is badly eroded and uneven in places so watch your step. At the top of the hill turn right crossing 24th Street and heading

Looking south from Raven Rocks viewpoint

east on a paved path (2.9 km). This is where the detour route rejoins the main route. You are now on the south side of the community of Woodlands.

The route stays on the path along the top of the escarpment going past a junction where a trail to the right leads down the slope into the park. The path makes a left turn and heads north on the west side of a heavily treed ravine. At the junction at the top end of the ravine (3.9 km) turn right and head south along the east side of the ravine. When you reach a point where the path turns left look for a trail leading to the right to a viewpoint (4.7 km). From this viewpoint there is a good view of the Raven Rocks area of Fish Creek Park on the left.

From the viewpoint retrace the route back to the junction at the top end of the ravine. Turn right and walk between houses to Woodgreen Drive across from Woodlands School. Turn left and walk west to Woodpark Boulevard. Turn right and walk a few steps to the bus stop (5.4 km). The Woodlands Village strip mall is just a short distance north of this bus stop.

Bus Directions from the end of the route to the station:
Catch bus # 56 Woodbine at stop 9129 on northbound Woodpark Boulevard at Woodgreen Drive. Get off at stop 6461 at the station. Stop 9129 is 14 minutes from the station. The bus frequency is 30 minutes daily at mid-day.

Route Summary:

1. Catch bus # 56 Woodbine and get off at the stop on westbound Woodfield Road just west of Woodhaven Crescent on the left.
2. Walk in the same direction as the bus route and turn left on Woodhaven Bay.
3. At a T-intersection with Woodhaven Crescent continue straight ahead on a path between houses.
4. The path turns left behind the houses on Woodhaven Crescent.
5. By the last house on the left the path turns left and ends at a sidewalk on Woodhaven Crescent.
6. Follow the sidewalk to the right and turn right onto a trail before you reach Woodfield Road.
7. When the trail ends at Woodacres Drive turn right on the sidewalk.
8. Turn left off Woodacres Drive on a path leading between houses.
9. The path leads down the slope to Bebo Grove. Stay left at two junctions on the slope.
10. When the path reaches the Bebo Grove access road turn left and follow the trail up the hill on the west side of the access road.
11. At the top of the hill turn right crossing the access road and walking east on a path along the top of the escarpment.
12. Stay on the main path ignoring a trail leading down the escarpment.
13. The path turns left and heads north along the west side of a ravine.
14. At the junction by the top end of the ravine turn right along the east side of the ravine.
15. At a junction where the path turns left follow a trail to the right leading to a viewpoint.
16. From the viewpoint retrace your steps back to the top end of the ravine.
17. Turn right at the junction and walk north between houses to Woodgreen Drive across from Woodlands School.
18. Turn left and walk west to Woodpark Boulevard.
19. Turn right and walk a few steps to the bus stop.
20. Catch bus # 56 Woodbine back to the station.

Anderson Walk 2
Douglasdale Pathway

Walk Overview: A short walk from the bus stop leads to an excellent viewpoint at the west end of 130th Avenue overlooking the Bow River and Fish Creek Park. The route heads north down the escarpment into the natural area on the west side of Douglasdale Estates. Most of the route is linear with an out-and-back section towards the end of the walk. The route finishes with a short section in Douglasdale. Much of this route is isolated so use your own discretion about walking alone.

Length: 5.7 km

Route Description & Accessibility: The accessibility at the start of the route is poor as you descend the steep path down the escarpment slope north of 130th Avenue. There is no alternate route described in the text that avoids this steep path. At the bottom of the escarpment the route becomes relatively flat. The walking surface is a mix of sidewalks and paved paths. Near the end of the walk the route crosses a gravel parking lot.

Food and Drink: A gas station convenience store is located on Douglasdale Boulevard near the end of the route.

Washrooms: The only washroom facility is a portable toilet beside the ball diamonds partway through the route.

Map References: Clear-View – 66 & 50, MapArt – 185 & 184
Rand McNally – 86 & 85, Sherlock – 49 & 48

Route Category: Bus/Walk/Bus – Ride the bus to the start of the route and when finished the walk ride the bus back to the station.

Bus Directions from the station to the start of the walk:
Catch bus # 96 McKenzie at stop 7797. Get off at stop 7377 on the southwest corner of 130th Avenue and Mount McKenzie Drive. This stop is 25 minutes from the station. The bus frequency is 30 minutes daily at mid-day.

The Walk: After getting off the bus walk back to the corner at 130th Avenue and turn left, walking west on 130th Avenue to a T-intersection at Mount Douglas Point and Douglasdale Point (0.3 km). Douglasdale Estates on your right was developed in the 1980s. Mountain Park on your left is part of the McKenzie Lake community. McKenzie Lake is named for J. McKenzie, a native of Montreal, who settled in this area in 1882. The city annexed this area in 1970 with development of the community beginning in 1982.

Path north of 130th Avenue

West of the end of 130th Avenue an access path leads to a triangular shaped pathway junction with the Bow River Pathway. The left branch heads south along the top of the escarpment. The next walk in this chapter Walk 3 – McKenzie Lake Loop follows this path south. Your route turns right at the junction and heads north on the Bow River Pathway. Joining these two branches is a short section of path that completes the triangular shape. Within the triangle are benches. The large natural area across the river is Poplar Island, a part of Fish Creek Provincial Park. There is no public access to the island. A small channel of the Bow River on the far side of the island separates the island from the rest of the park. The communities of Deer Run, Deer Ridge and Queensland can be seen from the viewpoint. A smaller island can be seen to the left of the viewpoint at the base of the slope.

From the viewpoint begin walking north as the path soon starts to drop down the slope. There are large rocks on the right side of the path to stop the uphill slope from sliding onto the path. At the base of the slope there are two small bridges that cross over areas that can become wet during times of heavy rainfall or springtime snowmelt. The path is now close to the

Path north of Higgins Bridge

riverbank. The route soon reaches the parking lot for the two ball diamonds. There is a pit toilet nearby. An access road leads from the parking lot to Douglas Park Boulevard.

The path then crosses a bridge over a water channel leading to the river from the Douglasdale Golf Club (1.4 km). Look for waterfowl and birds along this section of the river. You might be lucky enough to spot some American Pelicans. A flower guidebook would also be handy to have on this walk.

After crossing a bridge over a backwater of the river the path makes a turn to the left to get back to the edge of the river. The path soon reaches Sue Higgins Bridge (2.5 km). Sue Higgins served as the alderman of ward 14 for 21 years. The bridge crosses to the far bank of the Bow River in the Mallard Point area of Fish Creek Park. The north end of Poplar Island is at Mallard Point. Canyon Meadows Walk 3 – Mallard Point to Eric Harvie Bridge passes by the other side of the bridge.

Continue north on the path from the bridge. Ignore any paths leading to the right into the community. The route passes through an area that shows signs of human disturbance with rocks and limited vegetation indicating a former gravel pit site. On the other side of the river the path ascends the slope from Fish Creek Park to the top of the escarpment behind houses in Diamond Cove.

The path turns to the right and reaches a major junction (3.2 km). The path to the right from the junction leads to a large parking lot for the Douglasdale Driving Range and some tennis courts. Follow the left branch as the path continues north. You will return to this junction later and follow the right branch.

You are now separated from the riverbank by a treed area. The path moves closer to the riverbank just north of a bend in the river. From here, head north past a fenced off electrical structure. On one walk along here a hawk was observed sitting on top of the electrical structure screeching at anyone passing by on the path.

The path goes under Ivor Strong Bridge on Deerfoot Trail. Ivor Strong began working for the City of Calgary as an assistant City engineer in 1944, becoming the commissioner of public works and utilities from 1952 to 1956. He served as chief commissioner from 1965 to 1971.

On a hot summer day a short rest in the shadow of the bridge might be in order. A short distance north of the bridge the route reaches a junction (4.0 km). The right paved path leads into the community of Douglas Glen. The left branch is a dirt trail continuing north along the edge of the river. At the time of writing the former gravel pit site in this area is being developed into the community of Quarry Park. As the community is further developed the dirt trail by the river will likely be paved. This route can then be extended further north on that path.

From the bridge retrace the route back to the junction by the parking lot for the driving range. An alternate route on the way back to the junction might be to explore some of the dirt trails between the paved path and the riverbank. However, be prepared for overgrown sections, with branches to duck under or step over and spider webs waiting to get you in the face.

From the junction turn left to reach the parking lot. Walk diagonally across the lot to the short access road called Douglas Range Road. Turn right onto Douglasbank Drive (5.0 km) and follow this road to the junction with Douglasdale Boulevard. Cross at the lights to the far side of the road. Turn right and walk south to the bus stop (5.7 km). Nearby is a service station with a convenience store.

Bus Directions from the end of the route to the station:
Catch bus # 96 McKenzie at stop 6502 on northbound Douglasdale Boulevard at Douglasbank Drive. Get off at stop 7797 back at the station. This stop is 16 minutes from the station. The bus frequency is 30 minutes daily at mid-day.

Route Summary:

1. Catch bus # 96 McKenzie and get off at the stop on the southwest corner at 130th Avenue and Mount McKenzie Drive.
2. Walk back to the corner and turn left walking west on 130th Avenue to a T-intersection at Mount Douglas Point and Douglasdale Point.
3. Follow the access path leading west from the intersection.
4. At a triangular shaped pathway junction turn right and follow the path north as it descends the escarpment slope.
5. At the base of the escarpment the path crosses two small bridges.
6. The route then passes a parking lot for two ball diamonds.
7. Cross a bridge over a water channel flowing to the river.
8. After crossing the bridge path turns left and returns to the riverbank.
9. The path soon reaches Sue Higgins Bridge.
10. Continue north from the bridge staying on the main path.
11. The path turns away from the river and reaches a major junction near a large parking lot.
12. Take the left branch at the junction.
13. Continue on the path until it passes under Ivor Strong Bridge.
14. From the junction north of the bridge retrace the route back to the junction by the large parking lot.
15. Turn left at the junction to reach the parking lot.
16. Angle to the right across the parking lot to a short access road called Douglas Range Road.
17. Turn right on Douglasbank Drive.
18. At Douglasdale Boulevard cross to the far side of the road and turn right to the bus stop.
19. Catch bus # 96 McKenzie back to the station.

Anderson Walk 3
McKenzie Lake Loop

Walk Overview: This walk starts in the same location as the previous walk. The route combines two linear sections with a loop. The route begins by heading south from 130th Avenue along the top of the escarpment. Near the 5 km point the route descends the escarpment slope and follows the edge of a road to reach the Bow River Pathway. Near the conclusion of the walk there is a climb up the escarpment slope. The section of the route beside the river is isolated so use your own discretion about walking alone.

Length: 8.7 km

Route Description & Accessibility: The section of this loop route along the top of the escarpment is relatively flat with some short ascents/descents. Accessibility is good until you leave the path and follow a dirt trail to reach a very steep dirt trail leading down the escarpment slope to the McKenzie Meadows Golf Course access road. No alternate route for this slope is included in the text. The path by the river has good accessibility. Near the end of the route there is a steep climb up the escarpment slope. There is also no described alternate route that avoids this slope.

Food and Drink: There are no food stores or restaurants along this route.

Washrooms: When the route reaches the path beside the river there is a pit toilet if you detour a short distance south under the Marquis of Lorne Trail (Highway 22X) Bridges into the Rotary Nature area of Fish Creek Park.

Map References: Clear-View – 62, MapArt – 185 & 195
Rand McNally – 93, Sherlock – 49, 55 & 54

Route Category: Bus/Walk/Bus – Ride the bus to the start of the route and when finished the walk ride the bus back to the station.

Bus Directions from the station to the start of the walk:
Catch bus # 96 McKenzie at stop 7797. Get off at stop 7377 on the southwest corner of 130th Avenue and Mount McKenzie Drive. This stop is 25 minutes from the station. The bus frequency is 30 minutes daily at mid-day.

The Walk: After getting off the bus walk back to 130th Avenue and turn left walking west to the end of 130th Avenue (0.3 km). At a T-intersection continue straight ahead on an access path leading to a triangular shaped junction at the top of the escarpment. Turn left at the path junction and head south. At the bottom of the escarpment slope is the Bow River. On the far side of the river is Poplar Island, part of Fish Creek Park.

Continue along the top of the escarpment for almost 2 km until you reach Patterson Homestead Memorial Park (2.2 km), a small ornamental park with benches and information plaques. This location on top of the escarpment became the homestead of Edward M. Patterson in 1882. Patterson purchased the property in 1888 from the Department of the Interior. In 1921 his son Kyle took over the farm. Kyle and his son Bob operated the farm from 1966 to 1979 when much of the land was sold. Bob Patterson continued to farm the remainder of the land until it was sold to Carma Developers Ltd. Bob Patterson donated the finished park in 1997.

Continue south along the escarpment ignoring any paths leading left into

Looking south from the top of the escarpment

the community. The route reaches a major 4-way pathway junction (3.2 km) where one path leads left into the community. The path on the right switchbacks down the escarpment slope to a pedestrian bridge. On the other side of the bridge is Burnsmead in Fish Creek Park. Canyon Meadows Walk 4 – Mallard Point to Bow Valley Ranch passes by the other side of the bridge. You climb up the path on this slope near the end of the walk.

Your route continues straight ahead on top of the escarpment. There are a few small descents and ascents with the remainder of the path being relatively flat. As the route nears the Marquis of Lorne Trail the path turns left away from the top edge of the escarpment and enters the community (4.7 km).

At this point you leave the path and continue south along a trail that stays on the top of the escarpment. The escarpment ends at a point overlooking Highway 22X (the Marquis of Lorne Trail) and an access road to the McKenzie Meadows Golf Course. Descend a rather rough trail down the slope to the edge of the golf course access road (5.0 km). Turn right and walk downhill along the edge of the road continuing past the entrance to the

Remains of the 2005 flooding

golf course. The road leads to a parking lot near the river. There is also the parking lot for Rotary Nature Park on the other side of Highway 22X that can be reached by going to the left under the two bridges. There is a pit toilet building beside that parking lot. The route for Somerset-Bridlewood Walk 5 – Chinook Rotary Nature Park is on the south side of the bridges.

Under the bridges is a 2007 artwork by Roger Gaudreau entitled *Tracking the Trail*. A plaque indicates that aluminum, granite and stone were used in the artwork. There is a similar piece of artwork on the other side of the river under the bridge that you pass on the Somerset-Bridlewood Walk 3 – Sikome Lake & Lafarge Meadows.

From the parking lot on the north side of the bridge turn right and start to follow the path north beside the river (5.7 km). On the right is the boundary fence for the golf course. The path through this area had to be rebuilt after the heavy flood damage in 2005. There are still signs of the effects of the flooding where branches are piled up against trees.

At the north end of the golf course the route reaches the pedestrian bridge that leads across the river to Burnsmead in Fish Creek Park (8.2 km). Turn right at the bridge and follow the path as it switchbacks up to the top of the escarpment (8.4 km). Cross over your earlier route along the top of the escarpment and follow the path east into the community. This path leads to Mountain Park Drive. Turn left and walk a short distance to the bus stop.

Bus Directions from the end of the route to the station:
Catch bus # 96 McKenzie at stop 7049 on southbound Mountain Park Drive just south of Mount Belcher Place (8.7 km). Get off at stop 7797 back at the station. This stop is 35 minutes from the station. The bus frequency is 30 minutes daily at mid-day.

Route Summary:

1. Catch bus # 96 McKenzie and get off at the stop on Mount McKenzie Drive just south of 130th Avenue.
2. Walk back to the corner, turn left and walk west on 130th Avenue to a T-intersection at Mount Douglas Point and Douglasdale Point.
3. Follow the access path west from the intersection.
4. At a pathway junction where the paths form a triangular shape with the Bow River Pathway turn left and head south along the top of the escarpment.
5. The route reaches a small rest area named Patterson Homestead Memorial Park.
6. Continue along the escarpment ignoring any paths leading left into the community.
7. At a major four-way junction continue straight ahead. The route returns to this junction near the end of the walk.
8. As the route nears the Marquis of Lorne Trail, the path turns left away from the top edge of the escarpment and enters the community.
9. Continue south on a trail that stays on the top of the escarpment.
10. When the escarpment ends descend a rather rough trail down the slope to a golf course access road.
11. Turn right and follow the edge of the road downhill continuing past the entrance to the golf course.
12. As the route nears the river you reach a parking lot.
13. Turn right and follow a path heading north beside the river.
14. At the north end of the golf course the route reaches the pedestrian bridge crossing the river to Burnsmead in Fish Creek Park.
15. Turn right and follow the path as it switchbacks up the escarpment slope to the four-way junction you passed earlier.
16. Continue straight ahead from the junction on the path going east into the community.
17. At Mountain Park Drive turn left and walk a short distance to catch bus # 96 McKenzie on southbound Mountain Park Drive just south of Mount Belcher Place.

Chapter Eight
Canyon Meadows Station

Station Information: The station is on the west side of Macleod Trail near 130th Avenue. Cantrell Drive parallels the track on the west side of the station. Canyon Meadows community is west of the station and Lake Bonavista Estates community is east across Macleod Trail from the station.

The South line opened between downtown and Anderson Station in 1981. In 2001 Canyon Meadows Station and Fish Creek-Lacombe Station were opened. Stairs, up and down escalators and an elevator at the north end of the centre platform connect to the upper level of the station building. A left turn at the upper level leads to a short overpass over the southbound tracks to reach stairs and a ramp leading down to the east side of Cantrell Drive a few steps north of 130th Avenue. A right turn at the upper level leads to a long pedestrian overpass across the northbound tracks and Macleod Trail to a park and ride lot and the bus stop area beside Lake Fraser Drive. The bus stop end of the overpass is at ground level. A sign on the platform has information about Derek Besant's artwork entitled *Skywalk* located on the side of the overpass.

The area where Canyon Meadows is located was annexed in 1961 with development starting shortly after. The community name is derived from the Fish Creek valley or canyon to the south of the district and the meadows where the district now stands. Lake Bonavista is primarily residential with a long thin strip of retail and office buildings extending south from Anderson Road to Canyon Meadows Drive on the west side of Lake Fraser Drive. The development of Lake Bonavista started in the late 1960s. Two man-made lakes in the community, Lake Bonavista and Lake Bonaventure, are for resident use only.

Four of the five walks in this chapter visit Fish Creek Park east of Macleod Trail. Walks 2, 4 and 5 all pass through the Bow Valley Ranch area of Fish Creek Park where there are several historic buildings.

Canyon Meadows Walk 1
Babbling Brook Park

Walk Overview: This short out-and-back route visits a very pleasant linear park in Canyon Meadows. Several bridges cross a small stream that flows through the park.

Length: 3.0 km

Route Description & Accessibility: The accessibility for this relatively flat route is good. Near the station there is a gradual ascent/descent on 130th Avenue. The walking surface for the route is a mix of sidewalks, grass and trails.

Food and Drink: There are no food stores or restaurants along this route.

Washrooms: There are no public washrooms along this route.

Map References: Clear-View – 54, MapArt – 184
Rand McNally – 82, Sherlock – 47

Route Category: Walk – The route starts and ends at the station (no bus is required)

The Walk: From the upper level of the station turn left and cross the overpass for the southbound tracks and descend the stairs to street level and the start of the route.

Walk a few steps straight ahead to reach Cantrell Drive. At Cantrell Drive take a few steps to the left and turn right on 130th Avenue. Walk west on 130th Avenue to 6th Street. Turn right and walk north on 6th Street to Canterbury Drive. Turn left and walk west past some condos on the right and turn right onto the grass in Babbling Brook Park (0.8 km).

Cross the grass past a small pool and begin walking north on a trail. The trail passes through a green space between houses crossing several bridges over the small stream that flows through the park. The trail ends at a fountain set in the centre of another pool beside 124th Avenue and Cannington Way (1.5 km). From this pool retrace the route back to the station (3.0 km).

Route Summary:

1. From the upper level of the station turn left and cross the overpass above the southbound tracks and descend the stairs to street level.
2. Walk straight ahead to Cantrell Drive.
3. Walk a few steps to the left on Cantrell Drive and turn right to follow 130th Avenue west to 6th Street.

Bridge in Babbling Brook Park

4. Turn right and follow 6th Street north to Canterbury Drive.
5. Turn left and walk past some condos on the right turning right onto the grass in Babbling Brook Park.
6. Cross the grass past a small pool
7. Follow a trail through the park crossing several bridges on the way to a second pool with a fountain.
8. From this pool retrace the route back to the station.

Canyon Meadows Walk 2
Parkland, Bow Valley Ranch & Glennfield

Walk Overview: The first half of this loop route is on top of the escarpment on the west and south sides of the Parkland community. The area now occupied by Parkland was annexed in 1961 with development starting in the mid-1970s. Near the halfway point of the route you descend the escarpment slope to the Bow Valley Ranch area of Fish Creek Park. The return route is in Fish Creek Park passing through the Glennfield area of the park and going under Macleod Trail, a CPR bridge, the LRT Bridge and

141

Canyon Meadows Drive before arriving back at the station. There are sections of the route that benefit from the shade provided by the trees along the top edge of the escarpment or beside Fish Creek. Other sections of the route are more open with little shade. There are good views from the top of the escarpment. Some sections of the route in Glennfield are more isolated so use your own discretion about walking alone.

Length: 12.3 km

Route Description & Accessibility: Most of this relatively flat route has good accessibility. The only section with poor accessibility is when you descend the escarpment slope from Parkland to Bow Valley Ranch. There is no alternate route described in the text.

Food and Drink: There are some restaurants near the start of the route. Annie's Bakery & Café at Bow Valley Ranch is open seasonally. The fare in this small historic building includes drinks, sandwiches and dessert items. The Ranche Restaurant adjacent to the visitor centre offers a fine dining experience. However, a visit here is probably best left for a day when you are not so casually dressed in your walking clothes and walking shoes/boots. Several picnic tables are located near the visitor centre at Bow Valley Ranch. There are also three picnic areas with large shelters in Glennfield.

Washrooms: The visitor centre at Bow Valley Ranch has washrooms open year round although the hours of operation may vary depending on the time of the year. Glennfield has washrooms open year round.

Map References: Clear-View – 55 & 59, MapArt – 184 & 194
Rand McNally – 83, 91 & 92, Sherlock – 47, 48, 54 & 53

Route Category: Walk – The route starts and ends at the station (no bus is required).

The Walk: From the upper level of the station turn right and follow a long pedestrian overpass across Macleod Trail to the bus zone and parking lot for the station. Follow the edge of the parking lot access road to Lake Fraser Drive (0.2 km). Turn right and follow Lake Fraser Drive south to Canyon Meadows Drive. Canyon Meadows Centre is on the right. Turn left at Canyon Meadows Drive and walk one block east past the south side of Fish Creek Village to the intersection of Canyon Meadows Drive and Bonaventure Drive. Cross at the traffic lights to the south side of Canyon Meadows Drive and turn left (0.9 km).

At this point a path begins along the top of the escarpment on the south side of Canyon Meadows Drive. Glennfield is to the right at the bottom of the escarpment slope. On the far side of the park at the top of the south escarpment slope is the community of Midnapore. This area is described in more detail in the Fish Creek-Lacombe Station walks. Shortly after passing

Cottage at Bow Valley farm, 1904-1905. Glenbow Archives NA-2961-8

the intersection with Acadia Drive a path leads down the escarpment slope into Fish Creek Park (2.3 km). Stay on top of the escarpment and follow the trail angling to the right away from Canyon Meadows Drive. Within a short distance the trail joins a path on the west side of Park Estates Drive. This path started a few steps east of where the trail started.

When Park Estates Drive ends at Parkside Drive turn right following the path on the west side of Parkside Drive. When Parkside Drive turns left and heads east the path moves away from the road and continues south behind the houses on Parkview Crescent (3.6 km). The next road the path will parallel is Parkvalley Drive. The path then makes a loop along the edge of Parkvista Crescent before rejoining the edge of Parkvalley Drive.

143

Just before the path reaches Parkridge Drive look for a paved path going down the escarpment slope (5.1 km). This is the only section of the route where accessibility may be challenging. At the end of this path the route joins the main east-west path through the park just to the west of Annie's Bakery & Café (5.6 km). Turn left and when the path splits in a few steps take the left branch. The right branch allows cyclists to avoid the pedestrian traffic between Annie's and the visitor centre. The photo on the previous page shows the building where Annie's Bakery & Café.

On the east side of Annie's is Artisan Gardens. The three main themes in the gardens are First Nations history, family and local natural environment. The website for The Ranche at Fish Creek Restoration Society lists the participating artists and sponsors. The *Egg Money* bronze sculpture by Don and Shirley Begg was unveiled in 2002 by the Honourable Dr. Lois Hole, the Lieutenant Governor of Alberta. This sculpture of a farm wife and her two children feeding their flock of chickens recognizes the dedication and hard work of pioneer women. The 2003 *Cochrane Legacy* sculpture in Cochrane of a farm wife feeding chickens is based on the *Egg Money* sculpture. Continue straight ahead to the front of Bow Valley Ranch House where The Ranche Restaurant is located.

Homesteader John Glenn built a log structure in this vicinity in the 1870s where he and his wife Adelaide operated a small trading post. The Glenns sold their land to the Dominion Government in 1879 for use as a supply farm. The Glenns then moved further west along Fish Creek settling in the area just east of Macleod Trail where they operated a farm and stopping house. Theodore Robitaille purchased the supply farm in 1883 leasing the land to the Hull brothers prior to selling the land to them in 1892. William Roper Hull named the farm Bow Valley Ranche in 1896 and hired architect James Wilson to design the ranch house which cost $4,000 to build. Hull developed a very successful irrigation system for his ranch, greatly increasing his crop production.

Patrick Burns purchased the land in 1902 renaming it Bow Valley Farm. The 6,800 hectares ranch extended north along the Bow Valley from Fish Creek to his packing plant in southeast Calgary. The foreman's house (now Annie's Bakery & Café) was moved to the farm from the M. Patterson ranch at Bayfield in 1904. The ranch continued to be operated by P. Burns Ranches Limited until being purchased by the Provincial Government in 1973 as part of the development of Fish Creek Park. A National Historic Site plaque is located along the path by the Ranch House.

The visitor centre with washrooms is just east of the ranch house (5.8

144

The Egg Money Sculpture at Bow Valley Ranch

km). At the visitor centre the park maps and information sheets are free. There is an interpretative area in the visitor centre outlining the history of the Fish Creek valley. From the visitor centre retrace your steps back to the junction just west of Annie's.

From here follow the path leading west across the open field. This is the main east-west path through the park so be aware of cyclists. Cross bridge # 10 and continue on the main path (6.4 km). Ignore a trail on the left that makes a loop before rejoining the main path. The route then comes to a four-way junction (7.1 km). Continue straight ahead on the path. The path leading uphill on the left passes between houses in Sundance on the left and Midnapore on the right. Fish Creek-Lacombe Walk 3 – Midnapore comes down this path. A trail on the right at the junction leads to a wetlands area. The area north of the main path near the junction was fenced off when the park first opened to protect a great blue heron nesting location that was used for many years.

The path then reaches a storm water pond that was developed after the extensive flooding in the park in 2005. Follow a trail to the right past the

Near Annie's Bakery & Café at Bow Valley Ranch

north side of the pond. After a few steps a trail on the right loops around the north side of another pond before rejoining the main trail you are on. Continue straight on the main trail. At the junction where the main trail is rejoined by the trail on the right there is another pond to your left. A couple of short trails on the west side of this pond lead back to the path. These trails are not shown on the Provincial Park map. Continue straight on the main trail. After a short distance the main trail meets a trail on the east side of a row of wooden utility poles that cross the park in a north-south direction. Turn right and follow this trail north to a junction with a path on the near side of bridge # 9 (8.6 km).

Ignore the right branch that leads across the bridge and up the escarpment slope to the south side of Canyon Meadows Drive to the path you were on earlier just east of Acadia Drive. Your route turns left on the near side of bridge # 9 and follows the path west to another junction (9.2 km). Ignore the path to the left from this junction that goes south back to the main east-west path. Your route turns right at the junction following a trail that will make a large curve to the left and head west beside Fish Creek. Follow the right branch at the next junction. The trail to the left leads to one of the picnic areas in Glennfield where there is a washroom building. The trail beside the creek will join the main east-west path just east of Macleod Trail (10.9 km). Turn right and follow the path west under the bridges of Macleod Trail and then under the bridges for CPR and the LRT.

Keep to the right side on this section of the path as the visibility is rather limited by several turns. Shortly after going under the last bridge there is a junction. Turn right and follow the path north across bridge # 8 (11.3 km). At the junction just beyond the bridge ignore the left branch that leads to the Votiers Flats area of the park. That section of path is on the Fish Creek-Lacombe Walk 1 – Evergreen Bluffs to Fish Creek-Lacombe Station. Your route leads right from the junction north of the bridge passing by a small scenic pond before going under Canyon Meadows Drive. Within a few steps the route is beside Cantrell Drive. Turn right and follow Cantrell Drive north to just beyond 130th Avenue (12.3). Turn right and climb the stairs or the ramp to the upper level of the Canyon Meadows Station.

Route Summary:
1. From the upper level of the station turn right and follow a long pedestrian overpass across Macleod Trail to the bus zone and parking lot.
2. Follow the edge of the parking lot road to Lake Fraser Drive.
3. Turn right and follow Lake Fraser Drive south to Canyon Meadows Drive.
4. Turn left and walk one block east on Canyon Meadows Drive to the intersection with Bonaventure Drive.
5. Cross to the south side of Canyon Meadows Drive at the traffic lights and turn left on a path.
6. Just beyond Acadia Drive stay left at a junction continuing on the path along the top of the escarpment.
7. Follow a trail to the right leading away from Canyon Meadows Drive.
8. The trail joins a path on the west side of Park Estates Drive.
9. Turn right as the path follows the west side of Parkside Drive.
10. The path then moves away from the road and goes behind the houses on Parkview Crescent.
11. The path will then be along the edge of Parkvalley Drive.
12. Follow the path along the edge of Parkvista Crescent before returning to Parkvalley Drive.
13. Just before Parkridge Drive turn right and follow a path down the slope to where it meets the main east-west path in Fish Creek Park just to the west of Annie's Bakery and Café.
14. Turn left and follow the path taking the left branch at a junction.
15. Follow this path as far as the visitor centre.
16. Retrace your steps back to the junction west of Annie's and walk straight ahead as the path heads west across an open field.

17. Cross bridge # 10 and continue on the main path.
18. At a junction with a path coming down the slope on the left continue straight ahead on the main path.
19. Turn right on a trail that leads past a pond on your left. Continue on this main trail until you reach a trail on the east side of a row of utility poles.
20. Turn right and follow the trail beside the poles north to bridge # 9.
21. Turn left at the junction before the bridge and follow a path west to another junction.
22. Turn right at this junction and follow a trail as it bends to the left and heads west beside the creek.
23. Stay on this trail until it reaches the main path just east of Macleod Trail.
24. Turn right and follow the path west under Macleod Trail and under the CPR Bridge and the LRT Bridge.
25. At a junction just west of the bridges turn right and follow the path north across bridge # 8.
26. A few steps north of the bridge take the right path at a junction.
27. The path passes under Canyon Meadows Drive before reaching Cantrell Drive.
28. Turn right and follow Cantrell Drive north to just beyond 130th Avenue.
29. Turn right and climb the stairs back to the upper level of the station.

Canyon Meadows Walk 3
Mallard Point to
Eric Harvie Bridge

Walk Overview: This out-and-back walk starts at Mallard Point in Fish Creek Park. The route goes north along the Bow River Pathway as far as Eric Harvie Bridge in Sue Higgins Park (formerly Southland Park) before returning back along the same route. The route ascends/descends long escarpment slopes at the north and south ends of the community of Diamond Cove. Canyon Meadows Walk 4 – Mallard Point to Bow Valley Ranch also starts at the same location as this walk. Some sections of this route are isolated so use your own discretion about walking alone.

Length: 11.2 km

Route Description & Accessibility: The first section of the walk in Mallard Point is relatively flat. However, the steep ascents/descents of the two escarpment slopes have poor accessibility. There is no alternate route included in the text. The walking surface is mostly paved paths with a few trails in the Mallard Point area.

Food and Drink: There are picnic tables at Mallard Point.

Washrooms: Mallard Point has a washroom building. At Sue Higgins Park there is a pit toilet building.

Map References: Clear-View – 56 & 50, MapArt – 185, 184 & 174 Rand McNally – 84 & 76, Sherlock – 48 & 42

Route Category: Bus/Walk/Bus – Ride the bus to the start of the route and when finished the walk ride the bus back to the station.

Bus Directions from the station to the start of the walk: From the upper level of the station turn right and cross the long pedestrian overpass above Macleod Trail to the bus stop area on Lake Fraser Drive. Catch bus # 28 Deer Run at stop 9155. Get off at stop 8306 on Deer Run Boulevard just south of Canyon Meadows Drive. This stop is 10 minutes from the station. The bus frequency is 30 minutes at mid-day on weekdays or Saturdays and 60 minutes on Sundays.

The Walk: After getting off the bus walk back to Canyon Meadows Drive and turn right. Walk a few steps east on the south side of Canyon Meadows Drive. The access road into the Mallard Point area of Fish Creek Park starts at the end of Canyon Meadows Drive.

North end of Poplar Island at Mallard Point

When the sidewalk ends follow a narrow path to a crosswalk where a wider path begins on the south side of the road. Follow this path a few steps to where it joins the main path. Turn left and follow the main path north. On your right is a narrow channel of the Bow River. For a short distance there is a trail between the path and the channel. The trail soon joins the path. On the other side of the channel is Poplar Island, part of Fish Creek Park. This large island extends south from Mallard Point to the Bankside area of Fish Creek Park. The island is closed to visitors.

The path leads to Mallard Point parking lot and washroom building (0.8 km). A few steps north of the washroom building there is a junction. Take the right branch and follow a path down a small slope into the Mallard Point picnic area. Within a few steps there is another junction. Take the trail to the right. The trail leads to the riverbank near where the channel branches off from the main part of the river at the north end of Poplar Island. The treed area across the river is on the route for Anderson Walk 2 – Douglasdale Pathway.

Follow the trail north along the edge of the river. The trail joins the path you left earlier just before Sue Higgins Bridge (1.3 km). This bridge is named for the former alderman Sue Higgins in recognition of her assistance in raising funds for the construction of this bridge.

The path continues north from the bridge past a boundary sign for Fish Creek Park. Walk up the escarpment slope on the east side of Diamond Cove. There is a bench at the top of the slope. The path continues north along the top of the escarpment to where it makes a turn to the left at the north end of Diamond Cove (2.7 km).

Turn right and follow a trail a short distance north from this turn to a viewpoint. Below the viewpoint is the major intersection where Deerfoot Trail, Anderson Road and Bow Bottom Trail converge. Return to the path and turn right. The path then turns right and goes down a long descent. At the bottom of the slope the path turns to the right again and then makes a left turn when it reaches the edge of the river.

The path goes under the Ivor Strong Bridge on Deerfoot Trail (3.7 km). John Ivor Strong worked for the city for many years in various capacities as assistant city engineer, commissioner of public works and utilities and chief commissioner. If it is a hot sunny day there is shade under the bridge.

Walk north on the path from the bridge to an area where the path goes through a narrow green space between the river on the right and a chain link fence on the left. Lafarge Cement is located on the other side of this fence. The path soon comes to a point where the company bridge was located. It allowed the trucks to cross to the gravel pit on the east side of the river. The area on the other side of the river is now being developed as the

Sue Higgins Park (formerly Southland Park)

community of Quarry Park. The company bridge was demolished after being heavily damaged in the flooding of 2005. The path in this area required major repairs after the flooding. An interesting feature in this location used to be the temporary closure of the path when a truck was crossing the company bridge. Gates would automatically slide across the path to stop pathway users while a truck was crossing the bridge. The gates would then open after the truck had finished crossing.

Continue north on the path leaving the company fence behind and enter a more open area. On the left is Riverside Golf Park. The path makes a couple of turns as it continues north in Sue Higgins Park (formerly Southland Park). This park is a very popular area with dog walkers. In the park a grove of trees has been named Tuckey's Grove to honour Nora Tuckey and her husband Sid. She was a strong advocate for the designation of the off-leash area in this park.

The path soon reaches a pathway junction at the west end of Eric Harvie Bridge. This is the turn around point for this walk (5.6 km). A path to the left leads past the parking lot and crosses over Deerfoot Trail. There is the option of walking a bit further north from the bridge on trails. Eric Harvie, a well-known Calgary lawyer, businessman and philanthropist, founded the Devonian Group of Charitable Foundations. The group was a major participant in the development of Calgary's river pathway system. Chinook

Walk 2 – Carburn Park and Riverbend passes by the east end of Eric Harvie Bridge. From the bridge retrace the route back to the start of the walk on Canyon Meadows Drive. Walk west to the bus stop on the north side of Canyon Meadows Drive just west of Deer River Gate (11.2 km).

Bus Directions from the end of the route to the station:

Catch bus # 28 Deer Run on westbound Canyon Meadows Drive at stop 8304. Get off at stop 9155 back at the station. Stop 8304 is 11 minutes from the station. The bus frequency is 30 minutes at mid-day on weekdays or Saturdays and 60 minutes on Sundays.

Route Summary:

1. From the upper level of the station turn right and cross the long pedestrian overpass above Macleod Trail to the bus stop area on Lake Fraser Drive.
2. Catch bus # 28 Deer Run and get off at the stop on Deer Run Boulevard just south of Canyon Meadows Drive.
3. Walk back to Canyon Meadows Drive and turn right on Canyon Meadow Drive. Walk a few steps east on the south side of Canyon Meadows Drive.
4. When the sidewalk ends follow a narrow path to a crosswalk where a wider path begins on the south side of the road. Follow this path a few steps to where it joins the main path. Turn left and follow the main path north. A trail on the right soon joins the path.
5. The path leads to the parking lot and a washroom building.
6. A few steps north of the building turn right on a path leading down a small descent.
7. In a few more steps there is another junction. Turn right on a trail.
8. Follow this trail along the edge of the river joining the path just south of Sue Higgins Bridge.
9. The path ascends an escarpment on the east side of Diamond Cove.
10. At the north end of the community the path makes a couple of turns before descending the slope.
11. After a couple of more turns at the bottom of the slope the path is again beside the river.
12. The path enters a narrow green space between the river and an industrial site fence.
13. The path then enters a more open area west of Riverside Golf Park.
14. The path reaches the turn around point at the west end of Eric Harvie Bridge in Sue Higgins Park.
15. From here retrace the route back to Canyon Meadows Drive and Deer Run Boulevard.
16. The bus stop is on the north side of Canyon Meadows Drive a few steps west of Deer Run Boulevard near Deer River Gate.

Canyon Meadows Walk 4
Mallard Point to Bow Valley Ranch

Walk Overview: This linear route starts from Mallard Point in Fish Creek Park. On the way to Bow Valley Ranch, the walk passes through the Bankside and Burnsmead areas of the park. The first section of the walk is along the edge of a Bow River channel that separates the park from Poplar Island. The island is within the park boundaries. There is no public access to the island. From Mallard Point to Burnsmead the route follows a trail beside the river. The path between Mallard Point and Burnsmead is more direct but less scenic as much of the time the path is travelling through open fields with no trees and limited views of the river. The water channel on the west side of the island is a great location for spotting birds. In the spring look for mother ducks and their families of ducklings.

Mallard Point is named for the ducks that can often be found along the channel. Watch for swallow-nesting holes in the side of the riverbank. The name of Bankside is derived from the location along the riverbank. Burnsmead is named for Patrick Burns, the second owner of Bow Valley Ranch. The land area occupied by the communities of Deer Run and Parkland was annexed by the city in 1961 with development starting in the late 1970s. Some sections of this route are more isolated so use your own discretion about walking alone.

Length: 6.3 km

Route Description & Accessibility: Most of this route has good accessibility along the relatively flat trail beside the Bow River. The trail can be uneven or possibly muddy in some locations. From the pedestrian bridge by Burnsmead to Bow Valley Ranch you follow a path. The route has poor accessibility when it climbs the slope behind the park visitor centre. There is no alternate route for this slope.

Food and Drink: There are picnic sites located at Mallard Point, Bankside and Bow Valley Ranch. Annie's Bakery & Café and The Ranche Restaurant are located near the visitor centre.

Washrooms: There are washrooms in Fish Creek Park at Mallard Point (year round) and Bankside (seasonal). The washrooms at Burnsmead are a bit of a walk from the path. The visitor centre at Bow Valley Ranch also has washrooms.

Map References: Clear-View – 66 & 59, MapArt – 185, 195 & 194 Rand McNally – 85, 93 & 92, Sherlock – 48, 49, 55 & 54

Route Category: Bus/Walk/Bus – Ride the bus to the start of the route and when finished the walk ride the bus back to the station.

Bus Directions from the station to the start of the walk:

From the upper level of the station turn right and cross the long pedestrian overpass above Macleod Trail to the bus stop area on Lake Fraser Drive. Catch bus # 28 Deer Run at stop 9155. Get off at stop 8306 on Deer Run Boulevard just south of Canyon Meadows Drive. This stop is 10 minutes from the station. The bus frequency is 30 minutes at mid-day on weekdays or on Saturdays and 60 minutes on Sundays.

The Walk: After getting off the bus walk back to Canyon Meadows Drive and turn right. Walk a few steps east on the south side of Canyon Meadows Drive. The access road into the Mallard Point area of Fish Creek Park starts at the end of Canyon Meadows Drive.

When the sidewalk ends follow a narrow path to a crosswalk where a wider path begins on the south side of the road. Follow this path a few steps to where it joins the main path. Cross over the main path to reach a trail beside the path. Turn right and follow the trail south (0.3 km). On the left is a narrow channel of the Bow River. On the other side of the channel is Poplar Island, part of Fish Creek Park. This large island extends south from Mallard

Near south end of Poplar Island

Old tree along the trail

Point to Bankside. The trail turns to the left and heads east. After a right turn the trail continues south to Bankside. Near Bankside the river channel rejoins the main part of the river at the south end of Poplar Island.

At Bankside (3.0 km) the picnic tables are located down a small descent from the washroom building and parking lot. Across the river from the picnic tables is a steep escarpment slope. From Bankside continue south on the trail beside the river. The trail will turn and head southwesterly. Just before Burnsmead pedestrian bridge the trail turns right and ends at the main path (3.9 km). There is a park map at the junction. The bridge connects to the far side of the river at the base of the escarpment slope below the community of Mountain Park. Anderson Walk 3 – McKenzie Lake Loop passes by the other end of the bridge.

From the park map continue west on the path. Ignore any trails leading left or right. You reach a junction beside a chain link fence. Your route stays to the left on the main path with the fence on your right. The path to the right from the junction leads to the Burnsmead parking lot and washroom building. Since the 2005 flooding a constructed wetlands area has been developed in the Burnsmead area to try to reduce damage from flooding.

The fence encloses the Fish Creek sewage treatment plant. At times the odour from the plant can be a bit strong. At the south end of the treatment plant fence, the path turns right away from the river heading west towards Bow Bottom Trail (5.2 km). Use caution crossing Bow Bottom Trail as this is the access road to Hull's Wood and Sikome Lake.

At a junction on the west side of Bow Bottom Trail turn right and follow the path north. You very quickly come to two more junctions. Take the right branch at both junctions. The left branch at the first junction is the main path that bypasses the area in front of the visitor centre. The right branch from the second junction crosses the access road to Bow Valley Ranch parking lot. The path then turns left and heads west through an area with a straight line of trees. The path leads to the front door of the visitor centre (5.7 km).

Nearby the centre are some picnic tables. Within the visitor centre are park maps and information, a small museum interpretive area, and washrooms. On the west side of the visitor centre is the ranch house built in 1892 by William Roper Hull and later purchased by Patrick Burns. West of

Group preparing for tennis on William Roper Hull Ranch ca. 1896-1899. Glenbow Archives NA-5090-2

The Ranche Restaurant in the ranch house is the Artisan Garden with numerous works of art. Annie's Bakery & Café is located to the west of the garden in one of the smaller historic buildings associated with the ranch. There are other historic buildings south of the visitor centre.

After exploring the area at Bow Valley Ranch follow a path up the slope on the east side of the visitor centre. At the top of the escarpment you are beside Parkridge Drive. Turn left and follow the path in a northwesterly direction to the bus stop located at the end of the route near where Parkridge Drive meets Parkvalley Drive (6.3 km).

Bus Directions from the end of the route to the station:
Catch bus # 83 Parkland at stop 6468. Get off at stop 9155 back at the station. Stop 6468 is 11 minutes from the station. The bus frequency is 30 minutes at mid-day on weekdays or on Saturdays and 60 minutes on Sundays.

Route Summary:

1. From the upper level of the station turn right and cross the long pedestrian overpass above Macleod Trail to the bus stop area on Lake Fraser Drive.
2. Catch bus # 28 Deer Run and get off at the stop on Deer Run Boulevard just south of Canyon Meadows Drive.
3. Walk back to Canyon Meadows Drive and turn right on Canyon Meadow Drive. When the sidewalk ends follow a narrow path to a crosswalk where a wider path begins on the south side of the road.
4. Cross over the main path to reach a trail beside a channel of the river.
5. Turn right and follow the trail.
6. The trail will turn left to head east.
7. The trail then turns right and continues south to Bankside.
8. From Bankside continue south on the trail beside the river.
9. The trail joins the path near the Burnsmead pedestrian bridge.
10. From the bridge follow the path west.
11. Take the left path at a junction beside the sewage treatment plant fence.
12. The path turns then right at the end of the fence and crosses Bow Bottom Trail. Make a right turn at the junction west of Bow Bottom Trail.
13. Take the right branch at the next two junctions.
14. After the last junction cross the access road to Bow Valley Ranch and turn left walking west past a straight line of trees.
15. The path leads to the front door of the visitor centre.
16. From the centre climb up the escarpment slope on a path starting on the east side of the visitor centre.
17. At the top of the slope the route is beside Parkridge Drive.
18. Turn left and walk to the bus stop located near where Parkridge Drive

meets Parkvalley Drive.

19. Catch bus # 83 Parkland back to the station.

Canyon Meadows Walk 5
Bow Valley Ranch & Hull's Wood

Walk Overview: This walk passes through Bow Valley Ranch and Hull's Wood in Fish Creek Park. The route is a mix of out-and-back, loop and linear sections. There are several historic buildings at Bow Valley Ranch. In Hull's Wood a portion of the route is beside the Bow River. Some sections of this route are more isolated so use your own discretion about walking alone.

Length: 6.5 km

Route Description & Accessibility: There is poor accessibility at the beginning and end of this walk on the descent/ascent of the escarpment slope on the north side of Fish Creek Park. Most of the remainder of the route is relatively flat on a walking surface of paved paths or trails. No alternate route for the escarpment slope is included in the text.

Food and Drink: Annie's Bakery & Café and The Ranche Restaurant are located near the Fish Creek Visitor Centre at Bow Valley Ranch. There are picnic tables at both Bow Valley Ranch and Hull's Wood.

Washrooms: At Bow Valley Ranch the washrooms are in the visitor centre. The washrooms at Hull's Wood are beside the parking lot.

Map References: Clear-View – 59 & 61, MapArt – 194 & 195 Rand McNally – 92, Sherlock – 54

Route Category: Bus/Walk/Bus – Ride the bus to the start of the route and when finished the walk ride the bus back to the station.

Bus Directions from the station to the start of the route: From the + 15 level of the station turn right and follow a long pedestrian overpass across Macleod Trail to the bus zone and parking lot for the station. Catch bus # 83 Parkland at stop 9155. Get off at stop 6468 at the terminal at Parkridge Drive and Parkvalley Drive. This stop is 10 minutes from the station. The bus frequency is 30 minutes at mid-day on weekdays or Saturdays and 60 minutes on Sundays.

The Walk: After getting off the bus start walking in a southeasterly direction along the top of the escarpment. Near Parkridge Green follow the

John Glenn's house, Midnapore ca. May 26th, 1885.
Glenbow Archives NC-12-1

paved path down the escarpment behind the Fish Creek Visitors Centre at Bow Valley Ranch. From the visitors centre (0.5 km) head south past the historic ranch cookhouse and bunkhouse buildings. The path crosses the access road to the ranch house before reaching the main path. Continue south on a path on the south side of the main path (0.7 km).

The path leads to bridge # 11 (0.9 km). Take the right branch on the far side of the bridge. At one time this small loop path used to have several locations where visitors could stop and listen to a short audio presentation. At the first turn in the loop after leaving the bridge there is a rather interesting feature. The side of the slope is undercut to form small cave-like locations. The gravel forming the roof of the caves has been cemented together by spring water depositing calcium carbonate causing the conglomerate of gravel to become the roof of the caves.

There is a bench here where one can pause and enjoy the sound of the creek flowing by. Continue along the loop to a path leading to the right on the east side of the loop. Follow this path as it crosses the main north-south path between Bow Valley Ranch and Sikome Lake. Within a few steps the path crosses Bow Bottom Trail (2.0 km) into the Hull's Wood area of the park. Use caution at this crossing. After crossing the road, turn right at the nearby junction and follow the path south.

At the second junction follow the path to the left. The right branch leads to the parking lot and the washroom building. At the third junction follow a trail to the left past a fenced off area where a portion of the previous path has been washed away by the creek. The trail is a short distance south of where Fish Creek joins the Bow River. The right branch path from this third junction is on the return section of this route. The trail will turn right and head south beside the river. There are a few picnic tables in this area. At the next junction with a trail on the right you stay to the left and continue to follow the trail south.

The route soon reaches a major junction with a paved path (3.1 km). This path will be on your return route. Turn left and follow the path south a large parking lot and a boat launch site (3.4 km). There are large information boards by the parking lot. From the parking lot, retrace the route back to the last junction and turn left following the path across an open field passing by the east side of the Hull's Wood parking lot. The route will rejoin the path at

Historic building at Bow Valley Ranch

Trail junction in Hull's Wood

the junction near where you turned left onto the trail. Turn left and retrace your steps back across Bow Bottom Trail and the north-south path to where you rejoin the loop path (4.9 km).

Turn right and complete the loop to bridge # 11. From here retrace your steps back to the visitor centre. Turn left walking past the front of the ranch house and past the Artisan Garden to reach Annie's Café. From this spot walk a few steps further west and turn right, following a path that leads up the slope to a point just south of Parkvalley Drive near Parkridge Drive. Turn right and walk a few steps to the bus loop at the intersection of the two roads (6.5 km).

Bus Directions from the end of the route to the station:

Catch bus # 83 Parkland at stop 6468. Get off at stop 9155 back at the station. Stop 6468 is 11 minutes from the station. The bus frequency is 30 minutes at mid-day on weekdays or on Saturdays and 60 minutes on Sundays.

Route Summary:

1. From the upper level of the station turn right and cross a long pedestrian

overpass above Macleod Trail to the bus zone area.

2. Catch bus # 83 Parkland and get off at the stop at the end of the route at Parkridge Drive and Parkvalley Drive.
3. After getting off the bus start walking in a southeasterly direction along the top of the escarpment.
4. Near Parkridge Green follow a path down the slope to the visitors centre.
5. From the visitors centre walk south across the grass past the two smaller historic buildings.
6. Follow a path that crosses the access road to the Bow Valley Ranch House parking lot and then reaches the main east-west path in the park.
7. Follow the path on the other side of the main path south to bridge # 11.
8. At the junction on the other side of the bridge turn right.
9. Follow this path as it makes a large loop going west and then turning east.
10. At a junction on the east side of the loop turn right on a path leading away from the loop.
11. This path crosses the main north-south path between Bow Valley Ranch and Sikome Lake.
12. The path then crosses Bow Bottom Trail into the Hull's Wood area where you make a right turn at a junction.
13. At the next two junctions take the left branch. After the second junction you are walking on a trail.
14. At the third junction stay left on the trail. At the next junction turn left onto a path.
15. This path leads to a large parking lot beside the boat launch site.
16. Retrace the route back to the last junction but this time go left on the path.
17. This path rejoins the earlier path you left by the fenced off area.
18. Turn left and retrace the route back across Bow Bottom Trail and the north-south path to the loop.
19. Turn right and follow the path to complete the loop back to bridge # 11.
20. Turn right crossing the bridge and retracing the route back to the visitor centre.
21. Turn left and walk west past the Bow Valley Ranch House and Annie's Bakery & Café.
22. Just west of Annie's turn right and follow a path leading up the escarpment slope to a point just south of Parkvalley Drive.
23. Turn right and walk a few steps to the bus loop.
24. Catch bus # 83 Parkland back to the station.

Chapter Nine
Fish Creek-Lacombe Station

Station Information: The station is on the west side of Macleod Trail beside Shawnee Gate. Fish Creek Park and Shawnee Slopes community are west of the station. Fish Creek Park and Midnapore community are east across Macleod Trail. At the south end of the centre platform there is handicapped access to the park and ride lot. Use caution crossing the tracks. From this end of the platform a set of stairs leads up to a long pedestrian overpass across Macleod Trail. From the north end of the platform a ramp leads up and over the southbound tracks to the bus stop area. Nearby there is a series of information plaques.

Shawnee Slopes is named for William and Helen Shaw. They emigrated from England in 1883 and settled in this area with their nine children. The family operated a woollen mill for many years. The Shawnee Slopes Golf Course was developed in 1965 on the Shaw's original homestead land.

Fish Creek-Lacombe Walk 1
Evergreen Bluffs to
Fish Creek-Lacombe Station

Walk Overview: This linear route begins in the Evergreen Bluffs area of the Evergreen community. The early part of the walk follows a paved path along the north side of Evergreen Bluffs on top of an escarpment slope overlooking Fish Creek Park. The route then descends the escarpment slope and passes through the Shannon Terrace, Bebo Grove, Votier's Flats and Shaw's Meadow areas of Fish Creek on the walk back to the station. Most of the route is through forest and is often close to or near Fish Creek. Much of the route is isolated so use your own discretion about walking alone.

Length: 11.2 km

Route Description & Accessibility: The accessibility of the path down the escarpment slope from Evergreen Bluffs is very poor. The path is so steep there is a barricade and signs suggesting cyclists walk their bikes down the slope. There is no alternate route that avoids this steep slope. From the bottom of the slope back to the station the route is relatively flat with a few small ascents/descents. Most of the route is on paved paths.

Food and Drink: Shannon Terrace, Bebo Grove and Votiers Flats all have picnic areas.

Washrooms: Shannon Terrace, Bebo Grove and Votiers Flats all have washroom buildings that are open year-round.

Map References: Clear-View – 53 & 54, MapArt – 184 & 183 Rand McNally – 81 & 82, Sherlock – 52, 46 & 47

Route Category: Bus/Walk – Ride the bus to the start of the route and walk back to the station.

Bus Directions from the station to the start of the walk:

Catch bus # 12 Southwest Loop at stop 9187. Get off at stop 4989 on southbound Everridge Drive just south of Fish Creek Boulevard. This stop is 13 minutes from the station. The bus frequency is 30 minutes daily at mid-day.

The Walk: After getting off the bus cross Fish Creek Boulevard to the north side and walk north on Evercreek Bluffs Gate to a T-intersection with Evercreek Bluffs Road. Follow a paved path in a green space on the north side of Evergreen Bluffs Road. Turn right at a junction to reach Evercreek Bluffs Way (0.6 km). Cross Evercreek Bluffs Way and follow a path between houses to a paved path on top of the escarpment on the north side of Evergreen Bluffs.

Turn left and follow the path west along the escarpment ignoring any paths or trails leading off the main path. Near the northwest corner of the community the path makes a right turn, passes a wetlands area (1.9 km) and descends the slope into the west end of Fish Creek Park. This is one of the steepest paths in the city.

At the bottom of the slope continue on the path crossing bridge # 1 over Fish Creek (2.5 km). Follow the trail to the right from a junction on the far side of the bridge. Within a few steps there is a second junction. Follow the left trail. This trail crosses a boardwalk over an area that tends to be wet. The trail will meet the right trail from the junction near the parking lot for the Shannon Terrace Environmental Learning Centre. The centre is located in the former home of a family that resided in this area prior to the creation of the park. Turn left when the two trails join and walk toward the learning centre.

Turn right and follow a path that goes by the south side of the learning centre. Make a left turn at the next junction going around the east side of the learning centre. On the right is a fenced off preservation zone (3.2 km). If snakes bother you, this will probably be your least enjoyable part of this walk. The hibernaculum behind the fence is where snakes gather in the winter to hibernate. There are two species of garter snake, wandering and red-sided, that live in this area.

164

Just north of the preservation zone the path joins the main east-west path through the park. There are picnic tables, washrooms and a parking lot nearby. Make a left turn and follow the path west to where the access road splits for the parking lot and the learning centre. Turn right, cross the parking lot access road and walk north on a trail. The trail leads to another parking lot with large information boards about the history of the park (3.7 km). East of the signs there was a large barn known as the Hilton Barn.

Joseph Shannon settled in this area in 1882, raising cattle on his Diamond Ranch. In 1911 he moved to California for health reasons. Two brothers, George and Bill Hilton, and their wives, Edna and Hazel, began renting the Shannon property in 1941. After their barn burned in 1942 they constructed a barn large enough to hold 60 cattle. The Hiltons operated a dairy until 1948. The Brand family then started renting the property for the next four years, operating a stable and a dairy. In 1952 the Shannon family sold the property. The new owners built the home that became the learning centre. They raised thoroughbred horses. Prior to the barn being demolished in 2003, a riding stable operated in the area.

Retrace your steps back to the picnic area and begin walking east. On the left you pass a small outdoor stage with seating. If your group has any prospective thespians this might be the spot for a short break while those group members present an impromptu performance.

Just beyond the stage is the historic Willans Barn (4.4 km). Norman Willans constructed this barn in the 1930s. He came to Canada from England in 1870 with his brother Bernard. In 1890 Norman moved to the Millarville area. Norman and his family then moved to the Fish Creek area in 1910 when he was appointed manager of the Bow Valley Ranch operated by Pat Burns. Norman and his wife Alice purchased the land east of the Shannon property in 1918.

Stay on the main path as it turns to the left and begins to head north to a four-way junction. Your route continues straight ahead from the junction. The right branch from the junction leads to bridge # 2. Prior to the extensive flooding in the park in 2005 there were three trail options on the far side of bridge # 2. The only trail left leads up the escarpment to the path you were on earlier at the top of the escarpment. A trail leading to Bebo Grove was closed after a bridge damaged in the 2005 flooding was not replaced. The third option was the Ridgeview Trail that traversed the escarpment slope. That slope was so heavily damaged by the flooding that the trail was closed permanently. The trail leading left from the four-way junction goes up the escarpment slope to the route for Anderson Walk 1 – Woodbine and Woodlands.

Willans Barn

As you follow the path straight ahead from the four-way junction it makes a large loop to the right beside the creek. This path was constructed after the flooding. Along this section of the route there is still evidence of the 2005 flooding and of more high water flow since then. When the path makes a major turn to the left you are near where the damaged bridge was located.

The main path soon reaches the Bebo Grove area of the park (5.7 km). Bebo Grove has a parking lot and a washroom building (open year round). A set of stairs south of the parking lot leads down to a picnic area by the creek. The area is named for Nelson Bebo. He squatted on this land from 1888 until 1899. Bebo farmed and hauled wood from the Tsuu T'ina land west of the park. Addison Hone, a wealthy settler from Ireland, purchased the property in 1905. Hone was an avid polo player, representing Fish Creek, Millarville and Calgary in competitions. Teams competed for the Hone Cup with games being played at the Fish Creek polo grounds, located in the open field east of the Bebo Grove access road. Hone returned to Ireland in 1918. The stone fireplace and chimney near the washroom building are all that remains of the house of a former resident. Anderson Walk 3 – Woodbine and

166

Evidence of erosion along Fish Creek

Woodlands passes by this parking lot.

From the Bebo Grove parking lot follow the path to the right leading east along the south side of the large field. The left branch cuts across the middle of the field. At the next junction turn right on the path leading south into the treed area south of the field. This path leads to bridge # 3 (6.3 km). On the far side of the bridge there was a trail to the right that led to the now closed Ridgeview Trail. Your route turns left on the far side of the bridge and within a few steps reaches a junction. Your route takes the left branch from the junction and heads north towards a four-way junction (7.0 km). The right branch from the junction leads up a small slope into an open area and a constructed wetlands built after the 2005 flooding. Fish Creek-Lacombe Walk 2 – Evergreen Estates passes the wetlands.

At the four-way junction continue straight ahead. The trail to the right from the junction climbs up the escarpment slope to the route of Walk 3 - Evergreen Estates. As you continue straight ahead from the four-way junction ignore any trails leading left and right on the way to bridge # 5 (7.2 km). Soon after crossing bridge # 5 you reach bridge # 6 (7.4 km). To the left

Set of stairs east of bridge # 6 leading up to Evergreen Estates

after crossing bridge # 6 are the south facing slopes of Raven Rocks. This is another park preservation zone with no access to the public.

On the far side of bridge # 6 there is a four-way junction. Take the left branch following a trail that stays closer to the creek than the centre branch path. The left branch trail and the centre branch path meet before you cross bridge # 7 (8.0 km). The right branch from the four-way junction by bridge # 6 leads up a set of stairs and climbs the slope to the route of Walk 2 – Evergreen Estates.

Cross bridge # 7 and follow the path to the right heading east from the junction. A trail to the left on the north side of the bridge leads up the slope to Woodlands. Stay on the path passing a wetlands area on the left and ignoring any trails leading to the right. As the route nears the Votier's Flats area turn right on a path. This path leads up a small ascent to some picnic tables and a washroom building overlooking the parking lot for Votier's Flats (9.1 km). This washroom building is not open year round. Bus # 3 turns around by the parking lot. Follow the path east from the washroom building down a short descent to the path on the west side of the parking lot.

Turn right and follow this path south down a gradual descent. Ignore the path going left at a junction. Walk a few steps straight ahead on a trail from the junction. On the left is a washroom building that is open year round. To the right is a network of trails with picnic tables scattered throughout the trees.

Follow the trail to the left just south of the washroom building as it heads in a southeasterly direction. The trail turns left and joins the path you left just before the washroom building. Turn right and follow the path to a junction just north of bridge # 8. This bridge is also on Canyon Meadows Walk 2 – Parkland, Bow Valley Ranch and Glennfield. Turn right and cross bridge # 8. At the junction on the far side turn right (10.3 km). Stay on this path until you reach a junction with a path leading left up a slope.

The Shaw's Meadow area west of bridge # 8 is where William and Helen Shaw settled with their family. Their woollen mill was destroyed by fire in 1917. The family played an important role in the community of Midnapore. They were active parishioners at St. Paul's Anglican Church. You pass this church on Walk 3 – Midnapore. The family name lives on in the communities of Shawnee Slopes and Shawnessy.

Turn left and follow the path leading up the slope. At a junction on this path turn left and within a few steps you reach Shawnee Rise (10.7 km). Follow this road south and turn left on Shawnee Drive. Walk east to the traffic lights on Shawnee Gate. Cross to the far side of the road and walk past the parking lot to the station (11.2 km).

Route Summary:

1. Catch bus # 12 Southwest Loop and get off at the stop just south of Fish Creek Boulevard on Everridge Drive.
2. Cross to the north side of Fish Creek Boulevard and walk north on Evercreek Bluffs Gate to a T-intersection at Evergreen Bluffs Road.
3. Continue straight ahead on a path taking a right turn at a junction and crossing Evergreen Bluffs Way.
4. Follow a path between houses and turn left on the path along the top of the escarpment ignoring any paths or trails leading off the main path.
5. Walk past a wetlands area and follow the path down the escarpment slope into Fish Creek Park.
6. Cross bridge # 1 and turn right on a trail.
7. Within a few steps take the left trail at a junction.
8. When the trails join turn left and walk towards the learning centre.
9. Turn right and follow the path on the south side of the learning centre.

S.W. Shaw's original log house 1884-85. Glenbow Archives NA-44-5

10. Make another left turn walking past the east side of the centre and walk a short distance north to reach the main east-west path.
11. Turn left and follow the path to a junction near where the access road splits for the picnic area and the Centre.
12. Turn right, crossing the picnic area road and follow a trail beside the access road to a parking lot with some information boards.
13. Retrace the route back to where you joined the main path and continue east past a small stage and an historic barn.
14. At a four-way junction continue straight ahead and follow the path all to the Bebo Grove parking lot.
15. From the parking lot follow the path along the south side of the open field turning right on a path that leads to bridge # 3.
16. Cross the bridge and turn left to reach a junction where you take the left branch.
17. Continue straight ahead at a four-way junction to reach bridge # 5.
18. Cross bridge # 5 and continue a short distance to bridge # 6.
19. After crossing bridge # 6 take a trail to the left.
20. The trail joins the main path just before crossing bridge # 7.
21. After crossing bridge # 7 follow the path to the right.
22. As the route nears Votier's Flats take a path to the right up a small

ascent to picnic tables and a washroom building.
23. Follow the path down a small slope towards the parking lot.
24. Turn right and follow the path to a junction. Take the trail to the right from the junction.
25. Turn left on a trail just past the washroom building.
26. When this trail turns left and joins the main path turn right.
27. At the next junction turn right to reach bridge # 8.
28. Cross bridge # 8 and turn right at the next junction.
29. Follow a path leading left up a slope to Shawnee Rise.
30. Turn left and follow Shawnee Rise to Shawnee Drive.
31. Turn left and follow Shawnee Drive to Shawnee Gate.
32. Cross to the east side of the road and walk past the bus stop area to the station.

Fish Creek-Lacombe Walk 2
Evergreen Estates

Walk Overview: This route begins on a path in Evergreen Estates. It then follows a trail along the north side of the community at the top of an escarpment slope on the south edge of Fish Creek Park. The route descends the slope on a rather rough trail before climbing back up the slope on the north side of Fish Creek Boulevard. Sections of this route are isolated so use your own discretion about walking alone.

Length: 3.8 km

Route Description & Accessibility: The accessibility is only good on the first part of this route. The trail along the top of the escarpment slope is a bit rough followed by the very uneven trail down the steep slope. There is no alternate route that avoids the steep slope.

Food and Drink: There are no stores or restaurants along this route.

Washrooms: There are no washrooms along this route.

Map References: Clear-View – 54 & 65, MapArt – 184 & 194
Rand McNally – 82, 81 & 89, Sherlock – 52 & 46

Route Category: Bus/Walk/Bus – Ride the bus to the start of the route and when finished the walk ride the bus back to the station.

Bus Directions from the station to the start of the walk:
Catch bus # 12 Southwest Loop at stop 9187. Get off at stop 9192 on westbound James McKevitt Road just west of Evergreen Street. This stop is 6 minutes from the station. The bus frequency is 30 minutes daily at mid-day.

The Walk: Start walking in the same direction as the bus route and turn right onto a path that heads west from James McKevitt Road. James McKevitt Road is named for one of the early residents of this area. At a T-intersection turn right and follow a path north between houses. At a four-way junction continue straight ahead to another T-intersection. Turn left and follow the path straight ahead at the next junction. Cross Evergreen Drive (1.0 km) and continue north through the community. At the next junction take the right branch.

Cross over Evergreen Hill (1.5 km) and follow the path as it turns left behind the houses backing onto the treed slope. When the paved path ends continue on a trail. Stay on the top of the escarpment passing two trails on the right.

The route then reaches a wider trail leading down the slope (2.2 km). This former road used to lead down to a residence in the Marshall Springs area of Fish Creek Park before the park was established. Stay left along the top of the slope until you reach the rather rough and steep trail leading down the slope into the park. At the bottom of the slope is a wetlands area. This feature was one of several wetlands added to the park after the extensive flooding in 2005. There is a junction at the base of the escarpment (2.6 km).

Your route follows the trail to the left along the south side of the wetlands. This trail can be muddy. The trail to the right from the junction leads to a

Wetlands at the base of the slope

Trail on the south side of the wetlands

another junction on the north side of the wetlands.

The path to the right from that junction leads down a slope towards bridge # 3. The left branch of the path leads along the north side of the wetlands and meets with the trail you follow on the south side of the wetlands (3.4 km).

When the trail and path meet, turn left and follow the path up the slope to a parking lot on the north side of Fish Creek Boulevard. Walk past the parking lot and turn right on the north side of Fish Creek Boulevard. At the intersection with Everbrook Drive, cross to the south side of Fish Creek Boulevard. Turn left and walk a few steps to the bus stop (3.8 km).

Bus Directions from the end of the route to the station:
Catch bus # 11 Southwest Loop at stop 9843 on eastbound Fish Creek Boulevard near Everbrook Drive. Get off at stop 9187 back at the station. Stop 9843 is 10 minutes from the station. The bus frequency is 30 minutes daily at mid-day.

Route Summary:
1. Catch bus # 12 Southwest Loop and get off at the stop on westbound James McKevitt Road just west of Evergreen Street.
2. Walk in the same direction as the bus route and turn right on a path going west from James McKevitt Road.
3. At a T-intersection take the path to the right.
4. Go straight ahead at a four-way junction and turn left at a T-intersection.
5. Follow the path going straight ahead at a junction and cross Evergreen

Drive. Turn right at the next junction and walk north crossing over Evergreen Hill.

6. The path leads left behind the houses. When the path ends follow a trail.
7. Ignore any trails leading right until you reach a trail leading straight ahead down the slope into a large open field with a wetlands.
8. Turn left and follow the trail along the south side of the wetlands.
9. When the trail joins the path at the west end of the wetlands turn left and climb the slope to a parking lot beside Fish Creek Boulevard.
10. Walk past the parking lot and turn right on the north side of Fish Creek Boulevard. At the intersection with Everbrook Drive, cross to the south side of Fish Creek Boulevard. Turn left and walk a few steps to the bus stop (3.8 km).
11. Catch bus # 11 Southwest Loop back to the station.

Fish Creek-Lacombe Walk 3
Midnapore

Walk Overview: This loop route starts by crossing a pedestrian overpass to the east side of Macleod Trail. South of the pedestrian overpass are two historic churches and a small cemetery. To the east of the churches across Bannister Road are several historic buildings on the former Lacombe Home site established by Father Albert Lacombe. St. Mary's University College is now located on this site. After a short walk along the south side of Fish Creek Park on the north side of the community, the route wanders through Midnapore before following the main east-west Fish Creek path on the way back to the station.

Midnapore was at one time a separate community south of Calgary. The area of Midnapore was annexed by the city of Calgary in 1961 with the development of the present day community of Midnapore beginning in the late 1970s. Donna Mae Humber's book *What's In a Name Calgary Volume II* mentions that there may be three possible origins for the name Midnapore. Each of the three origins is related to the city of Midnapore in India.

Length: 9.2 km

Route Description & Accessibility: Most of this route is on reasonably level paths with good accessibility. The most challenging area is a descent on the slope on the south side of Fish Creek Park.

Food and Drink: Glennfield picnic area is near the end of the route.

Washrooms: There are three washroom buildings in the Glennfield area.

Map References: Clear-View – 54, 55 & 58, MapArt – 184 & 194

Rand McNally – 90 & 91, Sherlock – 53 & 54

Route Category: Walk – The route starts and ends at the station (no bus is required).

The Walk: From the station platform cross the long pedestrian overpass to the east side of Macleod Trail beside Bannister Road. North of the overpass 145th Avenue connects Bannister Road to northbound Macleod Trail. Bannister Road is named for A.E. Banister (at times spelled Bannister), one of the Midnapore area's early residents. He started ranching in this area in 1884. Banister's son, Harold served as mayor of Midnapore in 1932 and 1933.

An access road leads from Bannister Road into the St. Mary's University College campus. St. Mary's purchased the land and established their campus on this historic Lacombe Home site in 1999. After speaking to St. Mary's staff about their privately owned campus, the advice received was to contact their office if you wish to enter onto the private property to view the historic buildings situated on the campus. The staff is agreeable to giving tours of the campus if you phone and make arrangements.

Under the direction of Father Lacombe the Lacombe Home opened in 1910. The facility was built to offer housing for orphans, the aged and the poor. The Sisters of Charity of Providence operated the facility. In 1963 the orphanage section of the home closed as the children were housed in smaller group-home settings. In 1969 the Sisters of Providence constructed the Father Lacombe Nursing Home building east of this location and moved the elderly residents to the new facility. In 2002 the name of the nursing home was changed to Father Lacombe Care Centre.

The original residential building was destroyed by fire in 1999. Historic structures remaining on the site include a brick laundry and frame shed dating back to about 1910, a wooden water tower and a brick carpenter's shop built in the 1920s, and a brick heating plant constructed in 1927.

From the end of the overpass turn right and walk across the grass towards the former St. Patrick's Roman Catholic Church, the first of two historic church buildings south of the overpass. This small wooden church was constructed in 1905 on land donated by the Glenn family. The first resident priest of the church from 1909 to 1916 was Father Lacombe. After the congregation moved to a larger building in 1983 the historic church became neglected and vandalized. St John Chrysostom Russian Orthodox Church, a new congregation formed in 2008, was looking for a place of worship. In 2011 the Russian congregation purchased the building and

Children playing outside Lacombe Home 1912.
Glenbow Archives, NA-3563-55

began the task of repairing and restoring the building.

From St. Patrick's take a few steps further south to St. Paul's Anglican Church (now called the Chapel of St. Paul's). This church was built in 1885 on land donated by the Glenn family. John Glenn, himself, was a very dedicated Roman Catholic. St. Paul's was constructed by the Midnapore Church of England Society. Reverend E. Paske Smith was the first minister from 1885 to 1888. The well-known Anglican minister Archdeacon John William Tims was rector from 1896 to 1898 and from 1916 to 1942. Pioneers Samuel and Helen Shaw were members of this church. Prior to the building of the new St. Paul's Church in Sundance in 1998, several descendants of early St. Paul's members re-established the Midnapore Church of England Society to make sure that the historic church and the nearby cemetery would be preserved on their present site. Before leaving the site of the two church buildings take some time to wander through the small cemetery (0.5 km). Many of the Midnapore area's early pioneers are buried here.

Continue the walk by exiting through the gateway on the south side of St. Paul's onto the west end of 146th Avenue. Turn left and walk east to Bannister Road. Cross Bannister Road and continue eastbound on 146th

Midnapore & Macleod Trail ca. 1914. Glenbow Archives NA-74-1

Avenue past the south side of St. Mary's University College. Use caution along this road as there is no sidewalk. Further east on 146th Avenue you pass Father Lacombe Care Centre. On the north side of the care centre building is the small white convent where the Sisters lived during the construction of the Lacombe Home. Near the convent is a small cemetery. During a Historic Calgary Week tour, participants had the opportunity to view the small convent and the cemetery. A large headstone in the cemetery has several names engraved on it. The nun giving the tour explained that some years ago a man stopped by and asked if he could earn some extra money by cutting the grass in the cemetery. However, in cutting the grass he had moved some of the headstones prior to beginning his work. Alas, there was no record of exactly where each moved stone was first located. The large headstone contains the names of the people whose headstones had been moved. The nun finished this story by saying that the man had done a very good job of cutting the grass.

Continue walking east on 146th Avenue until the road ends. From here continue straight ahead on a path in Fish Creek Park. A path will join your route from the left. At the next junction turn right and follow a path to Midridge Drive (1.9 km). Cross Midridge Drive and follow a path south past a playground and through a narrow green space between the houses on Midridge Rise on the right and Midglen Way on the left. Turn right on the north side of Midlake Boulevard and follow a path to the traffic lights at the intersection of Midlake Boulevard and Midridge Road.

Cross to the south side of Midlake Boulevard and walk south on an access road on the west side of Midnapore School to where a path starts. On your right are the Mid-Sun Community Hall and some playing fields. The path heads south across the field, turns right and leaves the playing field area, crossing over Midpark Crescent and entering a narrow green space. On the left are the houses on Midpark Crescent and on the right the houses on Midpark Drive. Cross Midpark Crescent a second time and continue through a narrow green space, making a left turn at a junction and crossing the north side of some playing fields to where the path ends at Midland Crescent.

Follow Midland Crescent east to Midlake Boulevard. On the left is the south fence of Midnapore Lake Centre. Turn right at Midlake Boulevard and walk south to the traffic lights at Sun Valley Boulevard. Turn left and cross the road to the east side of Midlake Boulevard. Follow the path on the left leading through a green space between Midnapore and Sundance (4.3 km). As the path enters Fish Creek Park it goes down the slope to a junction with the main east-west path through the park (5.1 km). Turn left and follow the path in a northwesterly direction. Canyon Meadows Walk 2 – Parkland, Bow Valley Ranch and Glennfield also follows this section of path. Continue on the main path until you reach the Glennfield area of the park. Each of the three main picnic areas at Glennfield has a parking lot, a large shelter, numerous tables and a washroom building. John and Adelaide Glenn settled in this area in 1879. Glenn developed Alberta's first irrigation system.

As the route nears Macleod Trail and the most westerly picnic area, turn left and walk south along the edge of the access road. Follow the access road to Bannister Road and turn left. Walk south to the intersection with 145th Avenue, cross to the west side of Bannister Road and cross the pedestrian overpass back to the station (9.2 km).

Route Summary:

1. From the station platform cross the long pedestrian overpass to the east side of Macleod Trail beside Bannister Road. The former Lacombe Home site is across Bannister Road from the overpass.
2. From the end of the overpass turn right and walk towards St. Patrick's Roman Catholic Church, the first of two historic church buildings south of the overpass.
3. From St. Patrick's take a few steps further south to St. Paul's Anglican Church.
4. Before leaving the site of the two church buildings take some time to wander through the small cemetery.
5. Continue the walk by exiting through the gateway on the south side of St. Paul's onto the west end of 146th Avenue.
6. Turn left and walk east to Bannister Road. Cross Bannister Road and continue eastbound on 146th Avenue.
7. Continue walking east on 146th Avenue until the road ends. From here

continue straight ahead on a path in Fish Creek Park.

8. A path will join your route from the left. At the next junction turn right and follow a path to Midridge Drive.

9. Cross Midridge Drive and follow a path south past a playground and through a narrow green space between the houses.

10. Turn right on the north side of Midlake Boulevard and follow a path to the traffic lights at the intersection of Midlake Boulevard and Midridge Road.

11. Cross to the south side of Midlake Boulevard and follow an access road on the west side of Midnapore School to where a path starts.

12. The path turns right and leaves the playing field area crossing over Midpark Crescent and entering a narrow green space.

13. Cross Midpark Crescent a second time and continue through a narrow green space, making a left turn at a junction and crossing the north side of some playing fields to where the path ends at Midland Crescent.

14. Follow Midland Crescent east to Midlake Boulevard.

15. Turn right at Midlake Boulevard and walk south to the traffic lights at Sun Valley Boulevard. Turn left and cross the road to the east side of Midlake Boulevard.

16. Follow the path on the left leading through a green space between Midnapore and Sundance.

17. As the path enters Fish Creek Park it goes down the slope to a junction with the main east-west path through the park.

18. Turn left and follow the path in a northwesterly direction. The path goes through the Glennfield area of the park.

19. Near Macleod Trail by the most westerly picnic area, turn left to reach the access road into Glennfield.

20. Follow the edge of the access road to Bannister Road and turn left.

21. Walk south to the intersection with 145th Avenue.

22. Cross to the west side of Bannister Road and cross the pedestrian overpass back to the station.

Chapter Ten
Shawnessy Station

Station Information: The station is south of Shawnessy Boulevard on the west side of Macleod Trail. The station is one of only two stations where the side loading platforms are staggered. A pedestrian crossing separates the two platforms. The staggered platforms at Martindale Station are separated by a road. Shawville Boulevard parallels the tracks on the east side. Shawnessy community is west of the station and the Boulevard Centre shopping complex is on the east side of the station. Shawnessy was established in 1981. The community is named for Samuel W. Shaw and his family who settled in 1882 beside Fish Creek to the west of what became Macleod Trail.

Shawnessy Walk 1
Shawnessy

Walk Overview: From the station this route follows pathways and sidewalks through the community. A portion of the route is in a green space between houses. An out-and-back section at the start and finish is connected to a loop. The main point of interest is an historic barn that is used as the community centre.

Length: 4.0 km

Route Description & Accessibility: The section of the route in the community green space has a gradual ascent on the out section of the walk followed by a gradual descent on the way back to the station. The loop section has a short steeper ascent followed by a short steeper descent.

Food and Drink: There are no stores or restaurants along this route.

Washrooms: There are no public washrooms along this route.

Map References: Clear-View – 58 & 57, MapArt – 194
Rand McNally – 90, Sherlock – 53

Route Category: Walk – The route starts and ends at the station (no bus is required)

The Walk: Walkers arriving on a southbound Somerset-Bridlewood train walk to the front end of the platform and turn right to reach the start of the route on the path on the west side of the station. Walkers arriving on a northbound Crowfoot train walk to the front end of the platform and turn left crossing both sets of tracks to reach the start of the route.

Begin the walk by turning left and heading south on the path. Look for the path leading right between the houses into the community green space (0.4 km). This first section of green space is narrow. On the right are the houses on Shawmeadows Road. On the left are the houses on Shawglen Rise. The green space widens as the route reaches the area beside an historic red barn (0.7 km). The McInnes Barn was constructed in 1915. John and Margaret McInnes and their family of four children settled in this area in 1905. John had spent a couple of years here during the 1880s before returning to Ontario. The family members were very involved in activities in the Midnapore area for many years. Another owner of the barn was Lowell Williamson and his wife, entertainer Dorothy McGuire. When the community of Shawnessy was developed in the early 1980s the developer converted the barn into the community centre.

In the area near the barn, there are tennis courts and a playground. From this location the path begins a gradual uphill climb in a northwesterly

McInnes Barn (now Shawnessy Community Centre)

direction. This area is pleasant with mature trees and large ornamental rocks scattered through the green space. On the right is Janet Johnstone School. The school opened in 1983. Janet Johnstone taught in five Calgary schools between 1942 and 1952. She was then appointed primary schools supervisor. From 1964 to 1973 she was assistant superintendent of elementary schools.

When you reach a major path junction (1.4 km) take the right branch as the path climbs a little more steeply up onto the playing fields on the south side of Father Doucet School. Father Leon Doucet arrived in Canada from France in 1868. Two years later he was ordained as a priest working in the area around St. Albert. He moved south to work with the Siksika and was living in the area close to where the NWMP crossed the Bow River in 1875 and established Fort Calgary. The path goes by the east side of the school. At Shannon Drive turn left and follow the sidewalk past the front of Father Doucet School.

Shawnessy Pathway

182

When Shannon Drive meets Shawinigan Drive (1.9 km) turn left and follow the sidewalk past Samuel W. Shaw School. South of the school turn left and follow a path back into the green space. In this area there are goal posts, an outdoor rink and a ball diamond.

There is a short steep downhill section as the route nears the earlier path junction where you turned right. Once you are back on the path at the junction (2.6 km), retrace the route through the green space and past the community hall on the way back to the station (4.0 km).

Passengers catching a northbound Crowfoot train cross both sets of tracks to the far platform. Passengers catching a southbound Somerset-Bridlewood train use the near platform.

Route Summary:
1. Begin the walk on the west side of the tracks by turning left and heading south on the path.
2. Look for the path to the right which leads into the community green space.
3. The green space widens as the route nears the area beside an historic red barn.
4. From this location the path begins a gradual uphill climb in a northwesterly direction.
5. At a major path junction take the right branch as the path climbs a little more steeply up onto the playing fields on the south side of Father Doucet School.
6. At Shannon Drive turn left and follow the sidewalk past the front of Father Doucet School.
7. When Shannon Drive meets Shawinigan Drive (1.9 km) turn left and follow the sidewalk past Samuel W. Shaw School.
8. South of the school turn left and follow a path back into the green space.
9. There is a short steep downhill section as the route nears the earlier path junction where you turned right.
10. Once you are back on the path at the junction retrace the route down through the green space past the community hall on the way back to the station.

Chapter Eleven
Somerset-Bridlewood Station

Station Information: The station is on the north side of Shawville Gate between 9th Street SW and Shawville Boulevard. Somerset and Bridlewood communities are west of the station. Somerset was established in 1995 and Bridlewood in 1998. Shawnessy Town Centre shopping complex is east of the station. The station has a centre platform. At the north end of the platform turn right to reach the park and ride lot and some of the bus stops. The remainder of the bus stops can be reached from the south end of the platform on Shawville Gate.

Somerset-Bridlewood Walk 1
South Fish Creek Pond

Walk Overview: This walk makes a circuit around a small pond on the south side of South Fish Creek Centre. Birds may be spotted in the area of the pond.

Length: 2.5 km

Route Description & Accessibility: Accessibility on this route is not great on the pond loop where the walking surface is rough and uneven. The remainder of the route is on sidewalks and grass. There is also a short descent/ascent near the pond.

Food and Drink: There is a food concession in South Fish Creek Centre. Several restaurants and coffee shops are close to the station.

Washrooms: There are washrooms in South Fish Creek Centre.

Map References: Clear-View – 58, MapArt – 194
Rand McNally – 91, Sherlock – 53

Route Category: Walk – The route starts and ends at the station (no bus is required).

The Walk: After getting off the train walk to the south end of the platform at Shawville Gate. Turn left and walk east to the traffic lights at Shawville Link. Cross to the south side of the road and continue straight ahead across the parking lot to the north side of Bishop O'Byrne High School. Paul O'Byrne was appointed Bishop of Calgary in 1968 at the age of 45. He died in 2004. The school is joined to the South Fish Creek Centre, home of the YMCA

West side of South Fish Creek Pond

Shawnessy. Turn left and walk along the north side of the school and the centre, going past the north entrance doors to the centre. Turn right and head south along the east side of the centre. After passing the east entrance doors you pass the arenas. At the south end of the arenas continue south on the grass. Go down a short slope to reach a gravel trail around the pond (0.8 km). The road south of the pond is Spruce Meadows Trail (Highway 22X). Make a clockwise circuit around the pond.

During the warmer months of the year, there are usually several species of waterfowl on the pond. Look for red-winged blackbirds along the edge of the pond. At the northwest corner of the pond, stop for a few moments and listen for a chorus of frogs. They are located in a wetland area beside the railway tracks. A fence separates you from this wetland.

Complete your circuit of the pond (1.7 km) and climb the small slope, walking north along the east side of the arenas. On your return walk back to the station, there is the option to enter the east doors and take a stroll through the centre. The centre has arenas, a swimming pool, gyms and a small concession. A public library is also in the building. Exit the centre by the north doors and head back to the station (2.5 km).

Route Summary:

1. After getting off the train walk to the south end of the platform at Shawville Gate.
2. Turn left and walk east to the traffic lights at Shawville Link.
3. Cross to the south side of the road and continue straight ahead across the parking lot to the north side of Bishop O'Byrne High School.
4. Turn left and walk along the north side of the school and South Fish Creek Centre, going past the entrance doors to the centre.
5. Turn right and walk south past the east side of the centre.
6. At the south end of the arenas continue south on the grass.
7. Go down a short slope to reach a gravel trail around the pond.
8. Make a clockwise circuit around the pond.
9. After completing the circuit retrace your steps back to the station.

Somerset-Bridlewood Walk 2
Bridlewood to
Somerset-Bridlewood Station

Walk Overview: This mostly linear route starts in Bridlewood in a community park. After an out-and-back section at Bridlewood Wetlands the route follows a paved path through Somerset back to the station. Bridlewood was established in the late 1990s. Bridlewood Wetlands, a 6 hectares site, on the east side of the community on the west side of James McKevitt Road, is probably the main point of interest on this route. There is a glacial erratic near the wetlands. Somerset to the east of James McKevitt Road was developed in the mid 1990s.

Length: 5.6 km

Route Description & Accessibility: This relatively flat route has good accessibility. The walking surface for most of the route is either paths or sidewalks.

Food and Drink: At the end of the walk there are several restaurants and coffee shops close to the station.

Washrooms: There are no public washrooms along this route.

Map References: Clear-View – 57 & 58, MapArt – 194
Rand McNally – 90, Sherlock – 52 & 53

Route Category: Bus/Walk – Ride the bus to the start of the route and walk back to the station.

Bus Directions from the station to the start of the walk:

Catch westbound bus # 14 Bridlewood at stop 8668 on the north side of Shawville Gate. Get off at stop 8521 on westbound Bridlewood Avenue just west of Bridlewood Drive. This stop is 16 minutes from the station. The bus frequency is 35 minutes daily at mid-day.

The Walk: From the bus stop start following a path north through Bridlewood Avenue Park. A point of interest is a line of older trees extending north through the park. It is probable that these trees were placed here as a windbreak by former owners of the land.

Staying on the main path, the route reaches a ball diamond on the left. Further to the left is Monsignor J.J. O'Brien School. John Joseph O'Brien was ordained at St. Mary's Cathedral in 1943. He oversaw the construction of the present St. Mary's Cathedral. Monsignor O'Brien was very dedicated in his work with immigrants.

From the pathway junction by the ball diamond turn right. This path soon

Bridlewood Wetlands

reaches Bridlewood Drive (0.6 km). Continue on the path on the east side of Bridlewood Drive. In a few steps there is another junction. Take the right branch. You will take the left branch later in this walk. As the path bends to the right you reach the north end of the Bridlewood Wetlands. In less than 100 metres, turn onto a trail on the right (0.9 km). The trail leads to a glacial erratic. This erratic was carried by a glacier from the area near Mount Edith Cavell in Jasper National Park.

Retrace your steps to the path by the wetlands and continue south. The path turns left and crosses a small bridge over the wetlands (1.1 km). The path then turns right along the east side of the wetlands. On the left is James McKevitt Road. In 1884 James McKevitt emigrated from Ireland and settled in the Midnapore area. He homesteaded 160 acres about 4 miles west of Midnapore near Red Deer Lake.

At the south end of the wetlands (1.5 km), turn around and retrace your steps back to the junction north of the wetlands. From here turn right and follow the path to the corner of James McKevitt Road and Bridlewood Road (2.5 km). Cross James McKevitt Road into the community of Somerset.

On the east side of James McKevitt Road there is a green space. Turn right and walk a few steps south. Turn left and follow the path leading east through the green space. At a junction in the green space take the right branch. This path ends at a T-intersection where Somerset Park meets

Children's Water Park at Somerset Square

188

Somerside Drive. Continue straight ahead along Somerside Drive to where it meets Somercrest Street at another T-intersection (3.2 km).

Turn right and follow Somercrest Street south to where it meets Somerset Drive a T-intersection. On the far side of this corner follow a path leading south between the houses. At the next junction take the left branch and head east. This path will bend to the right and lead to the north end of the field for Somerset School (3.89 km). Follow this path staying left at a junction. The path then turns left leaving the main field and entering a narrow green space.

At the next junction turn right and follow the path to reach Somerset Square. Cross the road into Somerset Square Park (4.3 km). This park has a children's water park, flower gardens, a playground and tennis courts. There is a metal sculpture in the park but no information plaque about the sculpture or the artist. The path turns right beside the tennis courts and heads south along the west side of the park. At the south end of the park cross Somerset Square and follow a path heading south between houses.

As this path reaches a more open green space it bends to the left. The path turns left as it nears 6th Street and follows the west side of the street north to the intersection of 6th Street and Shawville Gate. Cross to the east side of 6th Street and head east on the south side of Shawville Gate. You pass a park on the southwest corner of Shawville Gate and Somervale Court. Cross to the north side of Shawville Gate and continue east back to the station (5.6 km).

Route Summary:

1. Catch bus # 14 Cranston/Bridlewood on the north side of Shawville Gate.
2. Get off the bus on westbound Bridlewood Avenue just west of Bridlewood Drive.
3. From the bus stop start following a path north through Bridlewood Avenue Park.
4. From a pathway junction near a ball diamond turn right on a path.
5. Cross Bridlewood Drive and continue on the path to another junction.
6. Take the right branch.
7. At the north end of the wetlands follow a trail to the right to view a glacial erratic.
8. Retrace your steps and turn right on the path by the wetlands.
9. Turn left and cross a small bridge over the wetlands.
10. Near the south end of the wetlands turn around and retrace your steps back to the junction north of the trail leading to the erratic.
11. Turn right and follow the path to the corner of James McKevitt Road and Bridlewood Road.
12. Cross to the east side of James McKevitt Road and turn right, walking a

few steps to a path on the left. Follow the path east through a green space.

13. At a junction in the green space take the right branch.
14. The path ends at a T-intersection where Somerset Park meets Somerside Drive.
15. Walk east on Somerside Drive and at a T-intersection turn right on Somercrest Street.
16. Follow Somercrest Street south to a T-intersection with Somerset Drive.
17. On the far side of the street follow a path between houses.
18. At the next junction take the left branch and head east.
19. At the next junction on the north side of the school field take the left branch heading east.
20. The path turns left and enters a narrow green space.
21. At the next junction turn right and follow the path east to reach Somerset Square.
22. Cross the road into Somerset Square Park.
23. The path turns right by the tennis courts and heads south on the west side of the park.
24. At the south end of the park cross Somerset Square and follow a path between houses.
25. The path bends to the left and follows the west side of 6th Street north to the intersection with Shawville Gate.
26. Cross to the east side of 6th Street and follow Shawville Gate back to the station.

Somerset-Bridlewood Walk 3
Sikome Lake & Lafarge Meadows

Walk Overview: This walk begins on the east side of the community of Sundance on the top of the escarpment west of Fish Creek Park. The route is mostly out-and-back with one loop and some linear sections. After descending the escarpment, the route passes by the fenced off area around Sikome Lake. The route then heads south passing under Marquis of Lorne Bridge (Highway 22X) and follows the path south through Lafarge Meadows. From the south end of Lafarge Meadows retrace the route back to Sikome Lake and ascend the escarpment slope to reach the bus stop at the end of the walk. Parts of this route are isolated so use your own discretion about walking alone.
Length: 9.4 km

190

Route Description & Accessibility: The descent/ascent on the steep escarpment slope west of Sikome Lake has poor accessibility. The paths around Sikome Lake and in Lafarge Meadows are relatively flat. No alternate route is described in the text.

Food and Drink: There are picnic tables in the area around Sikome Lake. When Sikome Lake is open to the public there is a concession area.

Washrooms: When Sikome Lake is open to the public the washroom building is open.

Map References: Clear-View – 61, 72 & 63, MapArt – 194 & 195 Rand McNally – 92 & 100, Sherlock – 54 & 59

Route Category: Bus/Walk/Bus – Ride the bus to the start of the route and when finished the walk ride the bus back to the station.

Bus Directions from the station to the start of the walk: Catch bus # 78 Sundance at stop 6637 at the station. Get off at stop 7993 on eastbound Sun Valley Boulevard near the intersection with Sun Valley Drive. This stop is 12 minutes from the station. The bus frequency is 30 minutes daily at mid-day.

The Walk: Cross to the north side of Sun Valley Boulevard and start walking north on Sun Valley Drive. Within the first 300 metres, look for a trail on the right leading away from Sun Valley Drive. Follow this trail east to a viewpoint overlooking Fish Creek Park (1.0 km). Hull's Wood is straight ahead on the other side of Bow Bottom Trail. Sikome Lake is to the right from the viewpoint. On the other side of the Bow River the community of Mountain Park is at the top of the escarpment.

From the viewpoint descend the escarpment slope on a trail. This trail can be somewhat eroded and uneven so watch your step. At the base of the escarpment turn right on the path leading south towards Sikome Lake. On the left is Sikome Circle, the access road leading off Bow Bottom Trail. Your route arrives at a junction with a path descending the slope from Sun Valley Boulevard. Near the end of this route you will follow that path up the slope. Sikome Road, the vehicle access road from Sun Valley Boulevard, parallels the path leading up the slope.

Cross Sikome Circle (1.6 km) and walk across the grass towards the wire fence at the north end of the lake. Sikome Lake opened to the public in 1978. This man-made lake has a water surface of about 40 hectares. On hot summer days, large numbers of visitors gather here seeking some relief from the heat.

Turn left and follow the wire fence east and then south. When the path ends there is a short section where you walk across the edge of a grass slope beside the parking lot. In a short distance a path starts. Follow the path south through a treed area. There are some wetlands in this area. At a

191

Wetlands near Sikome Lake

junction turn left and follow the path east to Bow Bottom Trail (2.2 km). Ignore a trail to the right before reaching Bow Bottom Trail. On the other side of Bow Bottom Trail is a large parking lot. There are several interpretive signs beside the parking lot. That area is included in Canyon Meadows Walk 5 – Bow Valley Ranch & Hull's Wood.

Turn right and walk south along the edge of Bow Bottom Trail. There is no sidewalk or path in this area. There is very little vehicle traffic south of the parking lot unless Sikome Lake is open and visitors are using the south parking lot. The route reaches a closed gate on the north side of Marquis of Lorne Trail. The gate prevents vehicles from heading south. Walk around the gate and continue south, going under the two bridges on Marquis of Lorne Trail (2.6 km) into the Lafarge Meadows area of Fish Creek Park.

Under the bridges is a 2007 artwork by Roger Gaudreau entitled *Tracking the Trail*. A plaque indicates that aluminum, granite and stone were used in the artwork. The artist has a similar piece of artwork on the other side of the

Roger Gaudreau's *Tracking the Trail* under Highway 22X Bridge

river under the bridges.

A short distance south of the bridges, follow a path leading to the left along the riverbank. Lafarge Meadows, part of Fish Creek Park, is south of Highway 22X on the west side of the Bow River. A former gravel pit has been converted into a wetlands area of about 60 hectares. A golf course is west of Lafarge Meadows at the base of the escarpment. The community of Chaparral is west of the golf course with houses at both the bottom and top of the escarpment.

The Lafarge Meadows path has good views of the Bow River on the left and the wetlands on the right. Chinook Rotary Nature Park area of Fish Creek is on the east side of the river. At the top of the escarpment slope east of that park is the community of Cranston. Follow the path south through Lafarge Meadows. The turn around point is when the path reaches the south end of Lafarge Meadows (5.1 km). Retrace the route back to the access road for the south Sikome Lake parking lot. Turn left and follow the edge of the road to the parking lot. Turn right and walk north across the grass on the east side of the parking lot. Turn left and follow a path west along the north side of the parking lot. When the path ends cross a short section of grass and follow Sikome Circle north on the west side of Sikome Lake fence. When the road reaches Sikome Road turn right and walk a short distance to where you first crossed the road. Cross the road and walk a few steps north to reach the junction of the two paths. Turn left and follow the path up the slope on the north side of Sikome Road (8.8 km). When the path reaches Sun Valley Boulevard cross to the west side of that road and walk west a short distance on Sun Harbour Road to the bus stop (9.4 km).

Bus Directions from the end of the route to the station:

Catch bus # 78 Sundance at stop 6560 on westbound Sun Harbour Road just west of Sun Valley Boulevard. This stop is 13 minutes from the station. The bus frequency is 30 minutes daily at mid-day.

Route Summary:

1. Catch bus # 78 Sundance and get off at the stop on eastbound Sun Valley Boulevard near the intersection with Sun Valley Drive.
2. Cross to the north side of Sun Valley Boulevard and start walking north on Sun Valley Drive.
3. Within 300 metres turn right on a trail leading east to a viewpoint overlooking Fish Creek Park.
4. From the viewpoint descend the slope on a trail.
5. At the base of the escarpment turn right on a path leading south towards Sikome Lake.
6. At the junction with a path coming down the slope on the right leave the path and cross Sikome Circle and the parking lot towards the wire fence at the north end of the lake.
7. Turn left and follow the wire fence east and then south. When the path ends there is a short section where you walk across the edge of a grass slope beside the parking lot. In a short distance a path starts.
8. Follow the path south through a treed area.
9. At a junction stay left and follow the path east to Bow Bottom Trail.
10. Turn right and follow the edge of Bow Bottom Trail south passing under the two Marquis of Lorne Trail bridges.
11. A short distance south of the bridges turn left on a path.
12. Walk south on the path to the south end of Lafarge Meadows.
13. From the end of the path retrace the route back to the access road for the south Sikome Lake parking lot. Turn left and follow the edge of the road to the parking lot.
14. Turn right and walk north across the grass on the east side of the parking lot. Turn left and follow a path west along the north side of the parking lot.
15. When the path ends cross a short section of grass to reach Sikome Circle on the west side of Sikome Lake.

16. When the road reaches Sikome Road turn right and walk to the point where you first crossed the road. Cross the road and walk a couple of steps to reach the junction of the two paths.
16. Turn left and walk up the path on the north side of Sikome Road.
15. At Sun Valley Boulevard cross to the west side of that road and walk a few steps west on Sun Harbour Road to the bus stop.
16. Catch bus # 78 Sundance back to the station.

Somerset-Bridlewood Walk 4
Cranston Escarpment

Walk Overview: Most of this very scenic linear route is on the top of the escarpment on the west side of Cranston community. There are excellent views of both Chinook Rotary Nature Park at the base of the escarpment and across the river to Chaparral. The route finishes by making a loop around Cranston Pond on Cranston Drive. The community is named for the Cranston family who farmed in the area.

Length: 4.3 km

Route Description & Accessibility: With the exception of a short descent/ascent near Cranleigh Gate this relatively flat route has good accessibility. The walking surface is a paved path with short sections on sidewalks.

Food and Drink: There is a small strip mall near the start of the route. There are benches along the top of the escarpment.

Washrooms: There are no public washrooms along this route.

Map References: Clear-View – 63, MapArt – 195
Rand McNally – 101, Sherlock – 55 & 59

Route Category: Bus/Walk/Bus – Ride the bus to the start of the route and when finished the walk ride the bus back to the station.

Bus Directions from the station to the start of the walk:
Catch bus # 14 Cranston at stop 4994 on the south side of Shawville Gate east of the tracks. Get off at stop 4794 on Cranston Boulevard south of Cranleigh Drive. This stop is 12 minutes from the station. The bus frequency is 35 minutes daily at mid-day.

The Walk: After getting off the bus walk a few steps back to Cranleigh Drive and turn left. The small strip-mall is on the north side of the road. Walk

View from the Cranston escarpment

west on Cranleigh Drive to a T-intersection at Cranleigh Way (0.6 km). Cross to the west side of Cranleigh Way and continue straight ahead following a path between the houses. The path joins the main path along the top of the escarpment (0.8 km). The main path to the right soon ends and becomes a dirt trail.

Turn left and follow the path south. There is an excellent view from the top of the escarpment. Below you is Chinook Rotary Nature Park, a wetland area with several ponds that is part of Fish Creek Park. Somerset-Bridlewood Walk 5 – Chinook Rotary Nature Park describes a route around the wetlands. Beyond the ponds is the Bow River. The Lafarge Meadows area of Fish Creek Park is on the other side of the river. That area is visited on Somerset-Bridlewood Walk 3 – Sikome Lake and Lafarge Meadows. West of Lafarge Meadows on the south side of Highway 22A (Marquis of Lorne Trail) is the Chaparral community. Somerset-Bridlewood Walk 6 – Chaparral explores that community.

The path soon reaches the top edge of a ravine and turns left. Follow the path east to the edge of Cranleigh Way to get around the upper end of the ravine. The path leading down the ravine is on the route for Walk 5 –

196

Chinook Rotary Nature Park. The path along the top of the escarpment and the ravine path split from each other on the south side of the ravine soon after leaving the edge of Cranleigh Way (1.7 km).

The path turns left on the south side of the ravine and continues south along the top of the escarpment. Watch for a junction. Turn left off of the main path and follow a path to a playground on Cranridge Heights. The main path does continue further south but ends on the north side of Cranston Avenue.

From the playground on Cranridge Heights turn right and follow Cranston Heights north to Cranston Drive (3.2 km). Cross to the far side of the road and turn left. A few steps to the west near Cranwell Square is the bus stop at the end of the route (3.4 km). Before catching the bus there is the option of walking a loop on the paved path around the edge of Cranston Pond on the east side of Cranston Drive just north of Cranwell Square (4.3 km).

Bus Directions from the end of the route to the station:
After completing the loop of the pond catch bus # 14 Bridlewood at stop 9870 on westbound Cranston Drive at Cranwell Square. Get off at stop 8668 on Shawville Gate adjacent to the station. Stop 9870 is 16 minutes from the station. The bus frequency is 35 minutes daily at mid-day.

Route Summary:
1. After getting off the train walk to the south end of the platform.
2. Catch the eastbound bus # 14 Cranston on the far side of Shawville Gate east of the tracks.
3. Get off the bus at the stop on Cranston Boulevard south of Cranleigh Drive.
4. After getting off the bus walk a few steps back to Cranleigh Drive and turn left.
5. Walk west on Cranleigh Drive to a T-intersection at Cranleigh Way.
6. Cross to the west side of Cranleigh Way and continue straight ahead on a path between houses.
7. The path joins the main path along the top of the escarpment.
8. Turn left and head south on the main path.
9. The path reaches the top edge of a ravine and turns left.
10. Follow the path east to the edge of Cranleigh Way to get around the upper end of the ravine.
11. At the next junction take the left branch staying on the top edge overlooking the ravine.
12. The path turns left and continues south from the ravine.
13. At a junction take the left branch on a path leading to a playground on Cranridge Heights.
14. From the playground turn right and follow Cranston Heights north to

Cranston Drive.
15. Cross to the far side of Cranston Drive and turn left.
16. Turn right on a path making a loop around the edge of Cranston Drive Pond.
17. After completing the loop catch bus # 14 Bridlewood near the start of the path around the pond.

Somerset-Bridlewood Walk 5
Chinook Rotary Nature Park

Walk Overview: This walk descends through a ravine cut into the escarpment on the west side of Cranston. At the bottom of the escarpment the route makes a counterclockwise loop around ponds in Chinook Rotary Nature Park, part of Fish Creek Park. The Bow River flows by the west side of the park. Most of this route is isolated so use your own discretion about walking alone.

Length: 4.0 km

Route Description & Accessibility: The path down through the ravine is very steep with poor accessibility. There is no alternate route that avoids this slope. Part of the loop around the ponds is on a dirt trail.

Food and Drink: There are no food stores or restaurants along this route.

Washrooms: At the north end of Chinook Rotary Nature Park there is a pit toilet building just south of the parking lot.

Map References: Clear-View – 63, MapArt – 195
Rand McNally – 100, Sherlock – 55, 54

Route Category: Bus/Walk/Bus – Ride the bus to the start of the route and when finished the walk ride the bus back to the station.

Bus Directions from the station to the start of the walk:
Catch bus # 14 Cranston at stop 4994 on the south side of Shawville Gate east of the tracks. Get off at stop 8447 on eastbound Cranston Drive just east of Cranston Boulevard. This stop is 13 minutes from the station. The bus frequency is 35 minutes daily at mid-day.

The Walk: After getting off the bus walk back to the T-intersection with Cranston Boulevard. Continue straight ahead on Cranston Drive. The road

Path leading down to Chinook Rotary Nature Park

will bend to the left and head south. At the T-intersection with Cranleigh Gate, cross to the west side of Cranston Drive (0.5 km). Walk west on Cranleigh Gate to a T-intersection with Cranleigh Way (0.8 km).

Cross to the west side of Cranleigh Way to where the path leads along the top of the Cranston escarpment. Turn left on the path. In a few steps there is a junction where the left branch continues along the top of the escarpment. Follow the right branch down the ravine to Chinook Rotary Nature Park.

At the bottom of the slope there is a junction. Follow the trail to the right (1.4 km). The return portion of the route will be on the path to the left at the junction. As you walk north on the trail, the wetlands area is on the left and the escarpment slope is on the right. The Rotary Club of Calgary Chinook was instrumental in the development of this 16 hectares addition to Fish Creek Park. The wetlands area is located on the site of a former gravel pit. Watch for various types of waterfowl and birds in the area.

The park facilities include gazebo shelters, several benches and a pit toilet building. The trail joins the path just south of the parking lot near the pit toilet building (2.3 km). Access to this parking lot is from the north side of Highway 22X. The access road follows McKenzie Meadows Drive west from McKenzie Lake Boulevard. The route for Anderson Walk 3 – McKenzie Lake Loop follows McKenzie Meadows Drive on the north side of the bridge.

Chinook Rotary Nature Park

From the junction by the parking lot turn left and follow the path south back towards the bottom end of the ravine. The Bow River is on the right. After passing the junction at the south end of the park (3.1 km) begin the steep climb back up the ravine.

At the top of the ravine path turn left and walk back to the intersection of Cranleigh Way and Cranleigh Gate. Head east on Cranleigh Gate, cross to the far side of Cranston Drive and walk a few steps north to the bus stop (4.0 km).

Bus Directions from the end of the route to the station:
Catch bus # 14 Bridlewood at stop 9291 on northbound Cranston Drive at Cranleigh Gate. Get off at stop 8668 at the station. Stop 9291 is 14 minutes from the station. The bus frequency is 35 minutes daily at mid-day.

Route Summary:
1. Catch bus # 14 Cranston and get off at the stop on eastbound Cranston Drive just east of Cranston Boulevard.
2. Walk back to the intersection with Cranston Boulevard and continue straight ahead on Cranston Drive.

3. At the intersection with Cranleigh Gate on the right cross to the west side of Cranston Drive and follow Cranleigh Gate west to a T-intersection with Cranleigh Way.
4. Cross to the west side of Cranleigh Way and turn left on a path.
5. At a junction take the right branch leading down through the ravine.
6. At the bottom of the ravine turn right at a junction onto a trail.
7. Turn left and cross over a narrow connection between the two large ponds.
8. When the route reaches the path turn left and follow the path back to the bottom end of the ravine and retrace the route back to Cranleigh Way.
9. Walk east on Cranleigh Gate and cross to the far side of Cranston Drive.
10. Turn left and walk a few steps north to catch bus # 14 Bridlewood back to the station.

Somerset-Bridlewood Walk 6
Chaparral

Walk Overview: This route makes a loop through the community of Chaparral. The community was established in 1995. The early part of the walk follows paths and streets through the community. Towards the end of the walk the route follows a path along the top of the escarpment on the east side of the community.

Length: 5.7 km

Route Description & Accessibility: This relatively flat route has good accessibility on paths and sidewalks.

Food and Drink: There is a small strip mall at the end of the route.

Washrooms: There are no public washrooms along this route.

Map References: Clear-View – 61, MapArt - 194
Rand McNally – 99 & 100, Sherlock – 58 & 54

Route Category: Bus/Walk/Bus – Ride the bus to the start of the route and when finished the walk ride the bus back to the station.

Bus Directions from the station to the start of the walk: Catch bus # 78 Chaparral at stop 4941. Get off at stop 7982 on eastbound Chaparral Drive near Chapala Drive. This stop is 20 minutes from the station. The bus frequency is 30 minutes daily at mid-day.

The Walk: The bus stop is adjacent to St. Sebastian School. The school's Italian born patron saint joined the Roman army in 283 AD. He was executed for criticizing the Emperor's persecution of Christians. St. Sebastian is the patron saint of athletes and patron to all soldiers.

From the bus stop start walking west on Chaparral Drive. The route passes the main entrance of Lake Chaparral (0.7 km). This facility is restricted to community residents only. Just beyond Chaparral Cove make a left turn and follow a paved path south through a green space behind the houses. When the path ends turn right on Chaparral Cove and then left heading south on Chaparral Manor (1.2 km). Before reaching Chaparral Drive turn left and follow a path southeast through a green space between houses. Cross Chapala Point and continue southeast through the green space. When the green space ends at Chaparral Drive (1.7 km), turn left and then left again heading east on Chapala Gate.

At Chapala Grove turn right and after a few steps turn left, continuing east on Chapala Road. Turn left walking north on Chapala Drive (2.3 km). When the route reaches playing fields turn right and head east across these fields on the grass to the end of Chapman Place. Continue straight ahead from Chapman Place onto Chapman Close. At a T-intersection turn left heading north. Turn right and head east on Chapala Way.

Chapala Way leads to Chaparral Boulevard (3.0 km). Cross Chaparral Boulevard and continue east on Chaparral Ravine Way. Turn right onto 200 Chaparral Ravine View and then left at a T-intersection. At the end of this short road begin following a path leading to the left (3.4 km). This path will turn left around the top end of a ravine beside Chaparral Boulevard (3.8 km). The route then turns east along the north side of the ravine before turning left and heading north along the top of the escarpment. At the base of the slope on the near side of the Bow River is the Chaparral Valley area of the community. Lafarge Meadows in Fish Creek Park is east of the houses. Across the far side of the river is Chinook Rotary Nature Park in Fish Creek Park. On the top of the escarpment above the park is the community of Cranston.

The path along the top of the escarpment ends near the north end of Chaparral Ridge Circle (4.9 km). There is a trail leading down the escarpment to the path through Lafarge Meadows. From the end of the paved path retrace the route back along the top of the escarpment to Chaparral Ridge Road. Turn right and follow this road west to Chaparral Boulevard. Cross to the west side of Chaparral Boulevard. On the northwest corner of the intersection is Chaparral Corner strip mall. On the southwest corner a few steps from the intersection is the bus stop (5.7 km).

Looking east from Chaparral escarpment

Bus Directions from the end of the route to the station:

Catch bus # 78 Chaparral at stop 4778 on southbound Chaparral Boulevard south of Chaparral Drive. Get off back at the station at stop 9199 on westbound Shawville Gate west of Shawville Link. Stop 4778 is 13 minutes from the station. The bus frequency is 30 minutes daily at mid-day.

Route Summary:

1. Catch bus # 78 Sundance/Chaparral and get off at the eastbound stop on Chaparral Drive just east of Chapala Drive.
2. Walk west from the bus stop on Chaparral Drive.
3. Just beyond Chaparral Cove turn left on a path leading south between houses.
4. When the path ends turn right on Chaparral Cove and left on Chaparral Manor.
5. Before reaching Chaparral Drive turn left and follow a path south between houses.
6. Cross Chapala Point and continue on the path.
7. When the green space ends turn left on Chaparral Drive and then left

again walking east on Chapala Gate.

8. At Chapala Grove turn right and after a few steps turn left walking east on Chapala Road.
9. Turn left and walk north on Chapala Drive.
10. Turn right crossing some playing fields to reach the west end of Chapman Place.
11. Continue straight ahead on Chapman Place onto Chapman Close.
12. At a T-intersection turn left and after a short distance turn right onto Chapala Way.
13. Chapala Way leads east to Chaparral Boulevard.
14. Cross Chaparral Boulevard and continue straight ahead on Chaparral Ravine Way.
15. Turn right on 200 Chaparral Ravine View and at a T-intersection turn left.
16. At the end of the road follow a path leading to the left.
17. The path turns left and goes around the top end of a ravine beside Chaparral Boulevard.
18. The path turns east along the north side of the ravine and then turns left along the top of the escarpment.
19. The path ends at the north end of Chaparral Ridge Circle.
20. From here retrace the route back to Chaparral Ridge Road.
21. Turn right and follow Chaparral Ridge Road west to Chaparral Boulevard.
22. On the southwest corner of the intersection catch bus # 78 Chaparral back to the station.

Somerset-Bridlewood Walk 7
McKenzie Towne

Walk Overview: Inverness Pond and High Street in McKenzie are on this loop route. The T-shaped pond often attracts several kinds of waterfowl. High Street extending north from the pond has been designed to resemble a small town main street with visitors angle parking their vehicles.

Length: 5.0 km

Route Description & Accessibility: This relatively flat route has good accessibility. The walking surface is a mix of paths and sidewalks. There is one short section near the end of the pond loop that crosses a sloped grass surface.

Food and Drink: Near the end of the route on High Street there are several smaller restaurants or coffee shops and a grocery store. There are picnic tables in Promenade Park and beside the Inverness Pond path on Promenade Way.

Washrooms: There are no public washrooms on this route.

Map References: Clear-View – 60, MapArt – 195
Rand McNally – 95, Sherlock – 55

Route Category: Bus/Walk/Bus – Ride the bus to the start of the route and when finished the walk ride the bus back to the station.

Bus Directions from the station to the start of the walk:

Catch bus # 153 Copperfield on the south side of Shawville Gate. Get off at stop 5458 on eastbound Promenade Way across from Promenade Park. This stop is 19 minutes from the station. The bus frequency is 35 minutes at mid-day on weekdays and Saturdays and 70 minutes on Sundays.

The Walk: After getting off the bus walk a few steps towards Inverness Pond to where several benches overlook the T-shaped pond. Across the road is the half-circle shaped Promenade Park at the south end of High Street.

From the benches continue along the path in a clockwise direction as it loops around the right hand side on the pond at the top of the T (0.5 km). Walk in a southwesterly direction along the lower portion of the T. There are usually waterfowl to observe in the water. Red-winged blackbirds often occupy the bushes and shrubs along the pond's edge. On one visit here, an American Goldfinch was spotted. As the vegetation along the edge of the pond grows it is providing extra protection and shelter for the birds and waterfowl.

At the south end of the pond (1.2 km), turn left and follow a path leading between houses to Bellosguardo Park on McKenzie Towne Drive. At the top of a small hill in this park there is a structure with several archways. The intention would seem to be to try and replicate an ancient ruin. It might be a bit quirky but the arches give this playground park a unique look. There is a good view from the top of the hill beside the arches (1.8 km). Retrace the route from Bellosguardo Park back to the pond path. Continue the clockwise circuit. At the left hand side of the top of the T-shape the path ends and there is a short walk on a sidewalk. When the sidewalk reaches a back alley turn right and walk across the grass to reach the path beside Promenade Way (3.3 km).

Turn left and follow Promenade Way west one block to Inverness Square (3.4 km), a green space encircled by townhouses and condos. A gazebo sits in the centre of the park. Make a loop around the outer edge of the Square and walk east two blocks on Promenade Way turning left onto Inverness Gate (4.0 km).

Inverness Pond

When the route reaches a traffic circle follow the sidewalk around the edge of the circle in a counterclockwise direction. You pass a large white community church with a steeple. Fire Hall No. 30 is just past the church (4.3 km). The fire hall is an impressive brick building with a tower. On the far side of the traffic circle the town hall is also an interesting looking building.

From the traffic circle continue walking northeast on McKenzie Towne Boulevard and make a right turn onto McKenzie Towne Avenue. This road leads to the north end of High Street and a smaller traffic circle (4.6 km). A large chain grocery store is north of the circle. Turn right and head south along High Street. Developers have created a small-town atmosphere with the distinctive-looking fronts to the various businesses and shops along the two blocks of High Street.

Near the end of the route there is the option of purchasing a bite to eat in one of the businesses on High Street and continuing to Promenade Park at the south end of High Street. If it is a warm day, a table under a small gazebo roof provides some shade. The other option is to cross Promenade Way and choose a table overlooking Inverness Pond. An option for additional walking is to catch bus # 153 on the south side of Promenade Way at the

McKenzie Towne Fire Hall # 30

stop where you got off the bus. From this stop it is a 3 minute bus ride to the start of Walk 9 – New Brighton or a 7 minute ride to the start of Walk 8 – Copperfield Ponds.

Bus Directions from the end of the route to the station:

Catch bus # 153 Copperfield at stop 3921 on the north side of Promenade Way beside Promenade Park (5.0 km). Get off at stop 9299 on westbound Shawville Gate adjacent to the station. Stop 3921 is 14 minutes from the station. The bus frequency is 35 minutes at mid-day on weekdays and Saturdays and 70 minutes on Sundays.

Route Summary:

1. Catch bus # 153 Copperfield at the stop on the south side of Shawville Gate adjacent to the south end of the platform.
2. Get off at the stop on Promenade Way across from Promenade Park.
3. Walk a few steps towards Inverness Pond.
4. Turn left and start walking around the pond in a clockwise direction.
5. At the south end of the pond turn left and follow a path leading between houses to Bellosguardo Park on McKenzie Towne Drive.

6. From the park retrace your steps back to the pond.
7. Turn left and continue the circuit around the west side of the pond.
8. When the path ends nears the northwest corner of the pond take a few steps on a sidewalk and turn right walking across the grass to reach Promenade Way.
9. Turn left and follow Promenade Way west to Inverness Square.
10. Make a loop around the edge of the square and walk east on Promenade Way to Inverness Gate.
11. Turn left and follow Inverness Gate north to the edge of a traffic circle.
12. Turn right along the edge of the traffic circle, walk east on McKenzie Towne Boulevard and turn right on McKenzie Towne Avenue.
13. This road leads to the north end of High Street.
14. Turn right and walk south on High Street back to Promenade Way.
15. Catch bus # 153 Copperfield on the north side of Promenade Way next to Promenade Park.

Somerset-Bridlewood Walk 8
Copperfield Ponds

Walk Overview: This route passes three man-made ponds in the community of Copperfield. There may be waterfowl on one or more of the ponds. The direction of travel between the three ponds is roughly in a southwest to northeast direction. Most of the route is linear, finishing with a loop around the third pond.

Length: 4.1 km

Route Description & Accessibility: The paths and sidewalks offer good accessibility on this relatively flat route.

Food and Drink: There are no stores or restaurants along this route.

Washrooms: There are no public washrooms on this route.

Map References: Clear-View – 60, MapArt – 195
Rand McNally – 95 & 96, Sherlock – 56

Route Category: Bus/walk/bus – Ride the bus to the start of the route and when finished the walk ride the bus back to the station.

Bus Directions from the station to the start of the walk:
Catch bus # 153 Copperfield at stop 9299 on the south side of Shawville Gate. Get off at stop 3973 on southbound Copperfield Boulevard near Copperfield Garden. This stop is 26 minutes from the station. The bus frequency is 35 minutes at mid-day on weekdays or on Saturdays and 70 minutes on Sundays.

The Walk: After getting off the bus walk south to the intersection of Copperfield Boulevard and Copperfield Gate. Cross to the east side of Copperfield Boulevard to a community park. Follow a path east between two decorative wall-like structures and across a small bridge. At a T-intersection there is a sculpture of a child pulling a wagon with a teddy bear passenger. The sculpture entitled *Annie at Play* is by sculptors Don and Shirley Begg. A plaque dated 2003 recognizes the Hotchkiss family and Hopewell Residential Communities company for the donation of this sculpture.

A playground is on the left of the sculpture. Turn right and follow a path south away from the park into a green space between houses. At Copperfield Close cross the road and walk a few steps to the junction of the path around Copperfield Pond (0.4 km). As the vegetation around this pond matures the open water surface is being reduced. Turn right and follow the path crossing over a small bridge. The backs of houses encircle the green space around the pond. Near the southeast corner of the pond turn right and follow a path away from the pond to Copperfield Boulevard (1.0 km).

Bridge and sculpture at first Copperfield Pond

Turn left and follow Copperfield Boulevard northeast. After a gradual turn to the right the route reaches Copperleaf Link (1.4 km). Turn left and walk northeast to the end of Copperleaf Link where it meets Copperleaf Terrace. Cross the road and follow a path between houses to the path encircling Copperleaf Pond (1.6 km). This pond is roughly L-shaped.

Follow the path to the left around the north side of the pond. This left branch is the longer of the two branches around the pond. After passing the back of some houses the route passes a multi-unit housing complex and the park space surrounding the MDLCA Hall. Marquis of Lorne Community Association is an association of communities bordering Marquis of Lorne Trail (Highway 22A) located on the south side of Copperfield.

At the far end of the pond cross Copperstone Road (2.3 km) and continue walking in a northeasterly direction on Copperstone Boulevard. The route reaches an intersection with Copperfield Boulevard. Continue straight ahead on Copperpond Link. At a T-intersection follow a path between houses to the path around Copper Pond (2.9 km). Another sculpture is beside the path. This sculpture entitled *The Ollerenshaw Family* is of a man digging a hole to

The Ollerenshaw Family sculpture at the third Copperfield Pond

plant the tree held by a young boy. The plaque dated 2006 recognizes Hopewell Residential Communities company.

After making a loop of the pond (you choose the direction of travel this time) you return to the starting point. Walk back along Copperpond Link to Copperfield Boulevard. Turn right and walk a few steps to the bus stop (4.1 km). As mentioned in the previous walk you might wish to combine this walk with the McKenzie Towne Walk and/or the New Brighton Walk.

Bus Directions from the end of the route to the station:

Catch bus # 153 Copperfield at stop 9859 on westbound Copperfield Boulevard at Copperpond Link. Get off at stop 9299 back at the station. Stop 9859 is 27 minutes from the station. The bus frequency is 35 minutes at mid-day on weekdays and Saturdays and 70 minutes on Sundays.

Route Summary:

1. Catch bus # 153 Copperfield on the south side of Shawville Gate.
2. Get off the bus at the stop on Copperfield Boulevard near Copperfield Heights.
3. Walk to the intersection of Copperfield Boulevard and Copperfield Gate.
4. Cross to the east side of the road and walk straight ahead on a path between two decorative wall-like structures and cross a small bridge.
5. Turn right and follow a path south away from the park into a green space between houses.
6. At Copperfield Close cross the road and follow a path a few steps to a path around Copperfield Pond.
7. Turn right and follow the path to the right around the south edge of the pond crossing a small bridge.
8. Near the far end of the pond turn right and follow a path away from the pond to Copperfield Boulevard.
9. Turn left and follow Copperfield Boulevard turning left on Copperleaf Link.
10. Follow Copperleaf Link northeast to where it meets Copperleaf Terrace.
11. Cross the road and follow a path between houses to the path around Copperleaf Pond.
12. Turn left and follow the path around the north side of the pond.
13. At the far end of the pond cross Copperstone Road and walk northeast on Copperstone Boulevard.
14. At Copperfield Boulevard continue straight ahead on Copperpond Link.
15. At a T-intersection continue straight ahead on a path between houses.
16. Make a loop of the pond and retrace your steps back along Copperpond Link to Copperfield Boulevard.
17. Turn right and walk a few steps north to catch bus # 153 Copperfield back to the station.

Somerset-Bridlewood Walk 9
New Brighton

Walk Overview: This linear walk passes by New Brighton Pond.

Length: 2.1 km

Route Description & Accessibility: This relatively flat route has good accessibility. The walking surface is paved path and sidewalks.

Food and Drink: There are no food stores or restaurants along this route.

Washrooms: There are no public washrooms along the route.

Map References: Clear-View – 60, MapArt – 195
Rand McNally – 95 & 96, Sherlock – 55 & 56

Route Category: Bus/Walk/Bus – Ride the bus to the start of the route and when finished the walk ride the bus back to the station.

Bus Directions from the station to the start of the walk: Catch bus # 153 Copperfield at stop 9299 on eastbound Shawville Gate. Get off at stop 3939 on southbound New Brighton Drive near New Brighton Manor. This stop is 22 minutes from the station. The bus frequency is 35 minutes at mid-day on weekdays and Saturdays and 70 minutes on Sundays.

The Walk: After getting off the bus cross to the east side of New Brighton Way near the front of New Brighton Club. The use of this fenced-off facility is restricted to community residents. On the south side of New Brighton Club, follow a path east on the north side of Brightondale Parade. At a four-way junction continue straight ahead. At the second four-way junction the route is near the southwest edge of New Brighton Pond (0.7 km).

Turn left and follow the path along the west side of the pond. There may be waterfowl on the pond. When the route reaches New Brighton Drive turn right and head east along the north side of the pond. The route then leaves the edge of New Brighton Drive and follows the path as it curves around the east side of the pond.

At the southeast corner of the pond there is a tower-like structure near the water's edge (1.5 km). Continue west on the path along the south side of the pond to a three-way junction. The right branch leads to the junction where you started the circuit of the pond. Turn left and head south away from the pond. When the path reaches Brightondale Park follow the road south to New Brighton Drive. Turn right and walk west to the bus stop. There is the option to combine this short walk with Walk 7 – McKenzie Towne and/or Walk 8 – Copperfield Ponds.

212

Bus Directions from the end of the route to the station:

Catch bus # 153 Copperfield at stop 4993 on New Brighton Drive near New Brighton Green (2.1 km). Get off at stop 9299 back at the station. Stop 4993 is 20 minutes from the station. The bus frequency is 35 minutes at mid-day on weekdays or on Saturdays and 70 minutes on Sundays.

Route Summary:

1. Catch bus # 153 Copperfield and get off at the stop on New Brighton Drive south of New Brighton Gate.
2. Cross to the east side of New Brighton Way near the front of the New Brighton Club.
3. Follow a path along the north side of Brightondale Parade on the south side of the New Brighton Club.
4. At a four-way junction continue straight ahead on the north side of Brightondale Close.
5. The route reaches a four-way junction on the west side of the pond.
6. Turn left and follow the path around the west side of the pond.

New Brighton Pond tower

7. Turn right and walk along New Brighton Drive on the north side of the pond.
8. Turn right and follow a path around the east side of the pond.
9. Continue on the main path around the south side of the pond.
10. Near the southwest corner of the pond turn left on a path heading south away from the pond.
11. When the path reaches Brightondale Park follow the road south to New Brighton Drive.
12. Turn right to reach the bus stop.

Visitors to New Brighton Pond

Bibliography

Atkin, John. *Sky Train Explorer*. Vancouver: Steller Press, 2005.

Bullick, Terry. *Calgary Parks and Pathways – A City's Treasures*. Calgary: Blue Couch Books, 2007.

Foley, Jim. *Calgary's Natural Parks – Yours to Explore*. Calgary: Calgary Field Naturalists' Society, 2006.

Humber, Donna Mae. *What's In A Name ... Calgary?* Calgary: Detselig Enterprises Ltd., 1994.

Humber, Donna Mae. *What's In A Name ... Calgary? Volume 2*. Calgary: Detselig Enterprises Ltd., 1995.

Kwasny, Barbara., Peake, Elaine. *A Second Look at Calgary's Public Art*. Calgary: Detselig Enterprises Ltd., 1992.

Robertson, Anna. *Fish Creek Provincial Park*. Calgary: Rocky Mountain Books, 1991.

Sanders, Harry. *Calgary's Historic Union Cemetery: A Walking Guide*. Calgary: Fifth House, 2002.

Sanders, Harry. *Historic Walks of Calgary*. Calgary: Red Deer Press, 2005.

Walks by distance

3 km or shorter
2.1 km – Somerset-Bridlewood Walk 9 – New Brighton Pond
2.5 km – Somerset-Bridlewood Walk 1 – South Fish Creek Pond
3.0 km – Canyon Meadows Walk 1 – Babbling Brook Park

3.1 to 5 km
3.7 km – Victoria Park/Stampede Walk 3 – Mission 2nd & 4th Streets
3.8 km – Fish Creek-Lacombe Walk 2 – Evergreen Estates
4.0 km – Shawnessy Walk 1 – Shawnessy
4.0 km – Somerset-Bridlewood Walk 5 – Chinook Rotary Nature Park
4.1 km – Victoria Park/Stampede Walk 1 – Stampede Park & Elbow River Pathway
4.1 km – Somerset-Bridlewood Walk 8 – Copperfield Ponds
4.3 km – Somerset-Bridlewood Walk 4 – Cranston Escarpment
4.6 km – Erlton/Stampede Park Walk 1 – Reader Rock Gardens & Cemetery Hill
5.0 km – Somerset-Bridlewood Walk 7 – McKenzie Towne

5.1 to 7 km
5.4 km – Erlton/Stampede Walk 3 – Rideau Park & Roxboro
5.4 km – Anderson Walk 1 – Woodbine & Woodlands
5.6 km – Heritage Walk 1 – East Glenmore Park & Heritage Town Square
5.6 km – Somerset-Bridlewood Walk 2 – Bridlewood to Somerset-Bridlewood Station
5.7 km – Victoria Park/Stampede Walk 4 – Mission & Cliff Bungalow
5.7 km – Anderson Walk 2 – Douglasdale Pathway
5.7 km – Somerset-Bridlewood Walk 6 - Chaparral
5.9 km – Chinook Walk 3 – Lynnwood Ridge & Beaverdam Flats Park
6.1 km – Chinook Walk 1 – North Glenmore Park
6.2 km – Erlton/Stampede Walk 2 – Cliff Bungalow
6.3 km – Chinook Walk 4 –Ogden & Millican Estates
6.3 km – Canyon Meadows Walk 4 – Mallard Point to Bow Valley Ranch
6.4 km – Chinook Walk 2 – Carburn Park & Riverbend
6.5 km – Canyon Meadows Walk 5 – Bow Valley Ranch & Hull's Wood

7.1 km or longer
7.4 km – Victoria Park/Stampede Walk 2 – Ramsay & Scotchman's Hill
8.7 km – Anderson Walk 3 – McKenzie Lake Loop
8.9 km – 39th Avenue Walk 1 – Parkhill & Elbow Park
9.2 km – Southland Walk 1 – Palliser, Oakridge & South Glenmore Park
9.2 km – Fish Creek-Lacombe Walk 3 - Midnapore
9.3 km – Heritage Walk 3 – Weaselhead Flats Natural Area
9.4 km – Somerset-Bridlewood Walk 3 – Sikome Lake & Lafarge Meadows
10.1 km – 39th Avenue Walk 2 – Stanley Park, River Park & Sandy Beach
11.2 km – Canyon Meadows Walk 3 – Mallard Point to Eric Harvie Bridge

11.2 km – Fish Creek-Lacombe Walk 1 – Evergreen Bluffs to Fish Creek-Lacombe Station

12.3 km – Canyon Meadows Walk 2 – Parkland, Bow Valley Ranch & Glennfield

No distance listed
Heritage Walk 2 – Heritage Park

Walks by Category

Walk – Walk starts and ends at station (no bus required)
Victoria Park/Stampede Walk 1 – Stampede Park & Elbow River Pathway
Victoria Park/Stampede Walk 2 – Ramsay & Scotchman's Hill
Victoria Park/Stampede Walk 3 – Mission 2nd & 4th Streets
Victoria Park/Stampede Walk 4 – Mission & Cliff Bungalow
Erlton/Stampede Walk 1 – Reader Rock Gardens & Cemetery Hill
Erlton/Stampede Walk 2 – Cliff Bungalow
Erlton/Stampede Walk 3 – Rideau Park & Roxboro
39th Avenue Walk 1 – Parkhill & Stanley Park
39th Avenue Walk 2 – Stanley Park, River Park & Sandy Beach
Canyon Meadows Walk 1– Babbling Brook Park
Canyon Meadows Walk 2 – Parkland, Bow Valley Ranch & Glennfield
Fish Creek-Lacombe Walk 3 – Midnapore
Shawnessy Walk 1 - Shawnessy
Somerset-Bridlewood Walk 1 – South Fish Creek Pond

Bus/Walk – Ride bus to start of route and walk back to station
Somerset-Bridlewood Walk 2 – Bridlewood to Somerset-Bridlewood Station

Walk/Bus – Walk to end of route and ride bus back to station
Fish Creek-Lacombe Walk 1 – Evergreen Bluffs to Fish Creek-Lacombe Station

Bus/Walk/Bus – Ride bus to start of route and ride bus back to station from end of route
Chinook Walk 1 – North Glenmore Park
Chinook Walk 2 – Carburn Park & Riverbend
Chinook Walk 3 – Lynnwood Ridge & Beaverdam Flats Park
Chinook 4 – Ogden & Millican Estates
Heritage Walk 1 – East Glenmore Park & Heritage Town Square
Heritage Walk 2 – Heritage Park
Heritage Walk 3 – Weaselhead Flats Natural Area
Southland Walk 1 – Palliser, Oakridge & South Glenmore Park
Anderson Walk 1 – Woodbine & Woodlands
Anderson Walk 2 – Douglasdale Pathway
Anderson Walk 3 – McKenzie Lake Loop
Canyon Meadows Walk 3 – Mallard Point to Eric Harvie Bridge

Also by Peyto Lake Books

Walking Guidebooks
Walk Calgary's Escarpments & Bluffs (2005), $16.95
Calgary LRT Walks: The Northwest Stations (2013), $18.00

Calgary Parks
Discover North Calgary's Parks and Green Spaces (2006), $13.95
Discover Southeast Calgary's Parks and Green Spaces (2007), $12.95
Discover Southwest Calgary's Parks and Green Spaces (2008), $19.95

Banff Town Warden Journals
Banff Town Warden – 1914 to 1922 (2002), $19.95
Banff Town Warden 2 – 1923 to 1928 (2004), $19.95
Banff Town Warden 3 – 1929 to 1934 (2008), $19.95
Banff Town Warden 4 – 1935 to 1941 (2009), $19.95

Trivia Guides
Bill Peyto Guide to Canadian Rockies Trivia Volume 1 (2003), $10
Bill Peyto Guide to Canadian Rockies Trivia Volume 2 (2003), $10

Upcoming Publications
The author is currently working on Calgary LRT Walks: The Northeast
Stations and Calgary LRT Walks: The Downtown & West Stations

About the Author

David Peyto (Pea-toe) is a retired elementary school physical education
teacher with an interest in walking and history. Throughout his teaching
career he organized and lead walks for the students, fellow teachers and
parent volunteers. He is planning additional walking guidebooks. David and
his wife Linda live in Calgary.

NWMP building at Stampede Park

J.H.Woods Park on Elbow Drive

South Stations

Entrance to St. Mary's Cemetery

Carburn Park

South Stations

View from path near Rockyview Hospital

Heritage Town Square

Bridge over Bow River at Burnsmead

Glacial erratic at Bridlewood Wetlands